LOVE to EAT

HaTE to EAT

Elyse FITZPATRICK

HARVEST HOUSE PUBLISHERS
Eugene, Oregon 97402

Cover by Koechel Peterson & Associates, Minneapolis, Minnesota

LOVE TO EAT, HATE TO EAT
Copyright © 1999 by Elyse Fitzpatrick
Published by Harvest House Publishers
Eugene, OR 97402

Library of Congress Cataloging-in-Publication Data

Fitzpatrick, Elyse, 1950 –
  Love to eat, hate to eat / Elyse Fitzpatrick
      p.   cm.
  Includes bibliographical references.
  ISBN 0-7369-0013-6
  1. Eating disorders—Religious aspects—Christianity.
  2. Pastoral counseling. I. Title.
  RC552.E18F55   1999
  616.85'26—dc21   98-44305
                                                          CIP

Printed in the United States of America.

99 00 01 02 03 04 / BP / 10 9 8 7 6 5 3 2 1

Dedication

To my dearest friend, Julie Pascoe,
who was the first to touch my heart with Christ's love
and has since taught me of God's power to
keep His children through all their adversity.

Acknowledgments

I've been blessed beyond measure by family and friends who have continuously encouraged me to "follow on to know the Lord." Among these precious people are the members of my family, particularly my dear forbearing husband, Phil, who puts up with 15-minute dinners (on a good night) and encourages me in my ministry. My pastor, Dave Eby, and the members of North City Presbyterian Church (PCA) are so dear and have continually assured me of their love and prayers. Special thanks also to my dear sisters Anita Manata and Donna Turner, who have left little messages on my answering machine telling me that they're praying and are looking forward to seeing me again . . . someday. I'm also grateful for the women who have faithfully attended my Uncommon Vessels Bible studies and from whom much of the insight contained in this book has come. I must again thank Dr. George C. Scipione of the Institute for Biblical Counseling and Discipleship (IBCD) in San Diego for the way that he has patiently trained me to think about the sufficiency of God and His Word. I must also thank Jewelee Rossi (truly a jewel) for her feedback on this manuscript; my devoted mother, Rosemary Buerger, for her willingness to edit the rough drafts; and Steve Miller from Harvest House for his rare vision for biblical counseling and great skill in editing.

Everything I possess was given to me by our Great God and His wonderful children. . . . Thank you, Father.

Contents

There Is Hope for You

Part One: A Renewed Focus

Part Two: Understanding Who You Are

Part Three: Embracing God's Methods for Change

THERE IS HOPE
FOR YOU

*F*or the first time in my life, I think that I'm finally free from the tyranny of food. I don't spend my day thinking about what I've eaten, what I will eat, or how much I weigh. I'm learning to replace these thoughts with thoughts of pleasing God and using my eating habits and my body to glorify Him. I've learned that although my weight does reflect, in some ways, what's going on in my heart, it's not the most important thing in my life. Loving God is. I'm so thankful that the Lord has changed me. I feel like I've been released from a sunless prison of hopelessness, fear, and bondage."

As I sat and listened to Jenny's testimony, I knew that God's grace had worked strongly in her. She had finally come to walk in the truth of Jesus' words *"life is more than food"* (Luke 12:23). This book is written for women who understand what Jenny means when she talks about the tyranny of food and weight.

It's written to encourage you that you can have hope because you can change. This change won't happen just because you chose to read this book. No, the hope for this change is based on something much more wonderful and awesome than this little volume. This hope rests on God. He alone is the heart-knower. Think of it . . . He truly knows you! And because He knows you so well, He can deeply transform you.

The principles presented here rest in the assured confidence that God's Word is powerful. The writer of Hebrews describes it in this way: "the word of God is living and active and sharper than any two-edged sword" (Hebrews 4:12). The Holy Spirit uses God's Word in your life to teach, reprove, correct, and train you in righteousness. You can have hope because the Word of God is true, powerful, and eternal.

In addition to the wonderful resource of the Word of God, you have the assurance that the God who inspired this Word is faithful to it. The prophet Isaiah knew this when he said, "So shall My word be which goes forth from My mouth; it shall not return to Me empty, without accomplishing what I desire, and without succeeding in the matter for which I sent it" (Isaiah 55:11). God has pledged Himself— His changeless being—that He will be faithful to carry out all His Word. He has also pledged that He will be faithful to you, especially in your struggle against sin and temptation.

As if this weren't enough, you can also rest in the knowledge that your Savior, Jesus Christ, has made the way for you to be completely freed from your sins. He has paid the just penalty for your actions and has opened up the way for you to live joyfully in His holy service. Whereas you were once in bondage to the world, the flesh, and the devil, you now can rejoice in your new life of freedom. The Holy Spirit, who lives within you, has been given to you to teach you about these things. He can apply the truth of God's Word to your heart. He can transform and sanctify you.

These truths about God, His nature, and His Word are why I can say to you, "You *can* have hope!" Although I've worked with women with eating disorders for a number of years and have had training in biblical counseling, I'm not asking you to put your trust in me or my ideas. And even though I've had to work through some of these same problems and have come to freedom in my life, I know that I can fail. There is only one source of true hope. There is only one place where you should put your confidence. It is in your loving, faithful, holy, and powerful Father. He has promised you the joy of His glorious presence. He's right there with you. He's brought you to this place in your life so that you can learn what it means to have His strength in your weakness. And while it is true that I may understand many of the issues you are facing today, and I hope to be the means that God uses to help you grow, ultimately, He is the source of your growth and change. Put your confidence in Him! He loves you and delights in helping you more than you will ever know.

This little book is *not a diet book*. You won't find any lists telling you what you may and may not eat. You won't find any recipes in the back of this book. If you're like me, you've read many *diet* books—and even some books that said they weren't diet books (but really were). I've read many diet books, and I've tried to practice the steps outlined—"Don't eat carbohydrates!" "Don't eat fat!" "Don't eat sugar!" "Watch your calories!" But, I've never discovered in any of these books the truth about how to eat in a way that pleases God. . . . And I've found myself buying a new book every year or so because it seemed that the last one just didn't work for long. I've searched and searched— hoping to find the magic answer to my problem. I've discovered that I've been looking for the wrong remedy. I've even failed to define my problem correctly. I've been look- ing for an outward change when all the while God wanted to change my heart.

I know that it would be easier for you if I just gave you a set of rules. *Just tell me what I can and cannot eat, and I'll do it*, you may be thinking. I'm going to resist the tempta- tion to do that and instead I'm going to do something more difficult . . . and yet I believe much more beneficial and rewarding for you. I'm going to attempt to share with you how I believe God wants you to think about food and your eating habits. I'm also going to give you a *grid of discernment*, possibly an entirely new way of thinking about food, so that you'll know how to eat in any situation in which you find yourself. This is my goal because I don't want you to have to buy another diet book in six months. I'm hoping for something better for you. So, please be patient. I'm not aiming for a quick fix. No, I'm aiming for a change of heart—and I believe that God can change even *your* heart because He loves you and wants to change you much more than you can imagine. Read this book expectantly and patiently—settle in for some real heart-change . . . yes, it can happen even to you.

PART ONE

A Renewed Focus

LOVE
*to*EAT

HATE
*to*EAT

1

FROM HEARTACHE TO
A SENSE OF PURPOSE

*"Whether, then, you eat or drink or whatever you do,
do all to the glory of God."*

—1 CORINTHIANS 10:31

I want you to know who I am and why I am so
interested in this topic. I want you to understand my journey—I'll bet we're really not very
different. Struggling with eating, dieting, and even bingeing
and purging has been an abiding part of my whole life. The
truth is that I have struggled with my weight for as long as I
can remember. Even as a child, I remember the embarrass-
ment of having to buy "chubby" clothes at the department
store; of never being able to dress or look like the other girls
("That's not a style that would look good on you, dear," the
saleswoman would say); of being the brunt of fat jokes (my
uncle asking me if I was going to subdivide and build
because I had so much acreage); and the humiliation of
knowing that others were looking at how much I was
eating. To add to all this, I grew up near the beach in
Southern California—and all of my friends wore bikinis

during the summer. I remember saving my money and buying one in ninth grade, thinking that I was going to lose weight so that I could wear it in the summer. I never did.

I know the heartache and devastation of being chronically overweight. This isn't something that just happened to me as a child. Even after I became a Christian as an adult, I would pray night after night that God would help me to lose weight. I would imagine how wonderful my life would be if I could just wake up thin the next morning. I read ads about liposuction and dreamt of the day when I could get a shot or take a pill and be instantaneously "normal." I would diet and diet and do well for a time only to find myself entrapped again. After I had my three children, the problem just seemed to get worse and worse. How could I weigh so much? How could I ever change? I would get depressed and—you guessed it—go eat to try to give myself some pleasure.

It wasn't until I began to understand that God had something more important in mind than merely my looking good that I started to change and be thankful. God has taken this struggle of mine and turned it into blessing. He's used it to get at strongholds of self-indulgence, worry, fear, and pride in my own heart and He's produced fruit from it that comforts and encourages others. Because I now have this perspective, I'm able to rejoice over God's goodness.

I'm writing this book because I know the despair of hopelessness. I know what it's like to start a diet and to get derailed from it, sometimes only making it a day or two. I know the shame of jealously looking at other women who wear a size 8. But I also know the joy of conquering this problem and of helping hundreds of other women do the same thing. I know that you may be thinking, *Yeah, but I'm different.* I always felt that way. My confidence in telling you that you can change is not because I think that I have all the answers. It's just that I know Someone who does. As you read through this book, you'll meet other women who have struggles just like you and you'll see that there is a God who really is faithful to free us and change us. You *can* have hope!

Marsha's Story

Marsha had practiced habits of bulimia since she was in high school. She had been troubled by her gradual weight gain in the ninth and tenth grades, and although she tried to diet, she just couldn't seem to resist her favorite foods. She didn't want to leave her friends when they went out for french fries after class, but she knew she couldn't resist the food, either. So, she began to force herself to vomit whenever she ate something that she thought she shouldn't eat. As the years passed, Marsha continued to use vomiting (along with laxatives and diuretics) to try to control her weight. Because she knew that she could always "get rid of it," Marsha would sometimes go on a binge and eat incredible amounts of food in a short period of time.

The youngest of three sisters, Marsha's motivation was to stay as thin as her siblings. So even after marriage and childbirth, she continued her practices. At first she thought these behaviors were "no big deal," but eventually her body started to show the effects of her habits. Her salivary glands were swollen from the constant irritation of vomiting and her teeth were eroding from exposure to her stomach acids. As a Christian she thought that what she was doing was wrong, but she just didn't know how to stop. She had tried to quit scores of times, only to find herself once more standing over the kitchen sink in shame and helplessness, hoping that no one would discover what she had done. She, too, felt the despair of hopelessness. It seemed that her life was spinning out of control. Why couldn't she stop? She was disgusted with her behavior. Every time she threw up she was filled with shame and anger. Why couldn't she just get over this? Where was God?

Angela's Story

Angela had always been a compliant daughter and an above-average student. Although she fought from time to time with her mother, she was not rebellious. She seemed to love and respect her dad, who was the pastor of a large evangelical church. From all outer appearances, they seemed to be the perfect family.

One day, however, when Angela's mother happened to pass by Angela's room, she noticed Angelica's emaciated body, which apparently had been hidden by the clothes she wore. Terrified by the sight, her mother made an appointment with the family physician. "Anorexia? How could she have anorexia?" her mother and father asked when the physician dianosed the problem. It was then that Angela admitted to an intricate scheme of secrecy and dishonesty. When she had requested privacy, which included eating most of her meals in her room, it was to help hide her anorexic practices. Her parents had just chalked it up to adolescent behavior. They were aware that she was overly concerned about what everyone was eating and that she spent an enormous amount of time at the gym, but they had never imagined that their little girl was struggling with such a terrifying behavior. Why was she enslaved to this so-called desire for "perfection"? As the family talked, Angela admitted that she knew that what she was doing was wrong, but she just couldn't get herself to stop. Why couldn't she be like the other girls? Where had she gone wrong?

Different Yet Similar

The stories of Marsha, Angela, and me seem to be very different, don't they? Each one of us had what seems to be very different problems. Each of us were at different levels of natural and spiritual maturity. I was a Christian, yet I had a lifetime of habitually eating too much. Marsha, too, loved the Lord, but was enslaved to times of bingeing followed by purging and utter despair. Angela's commitment to Christ had always been part of what it meant to be her father's child, but now she struggled with an unquenchable desire to avoid any hint of weight gain. She had to be in control of every morsel of food and every ounce of weight. So in terms of our eating habits we were all very different, and yet all of us were totally consumed by the tyranny of food and eating.

If you struggle with any of these same problems I just mentioned, then you know what I mean when I refer to "the tyranny of food and eating." *Tyranny* is just the right word to use when it comes to the way many of us think about food, dieting, and our weight. Tyranny is oppression. It is enslavement. It means that we're dominated by thoughts and habits that torment and overpower. "What will I eat next?" "How much do I weigh today?" "What do others think of me?" "Why can't I get free of this?" "Why can't I be like others?" The same questions fill our thoughts over and over as we agonize day after day, looking for answers. Sometimes we try again; other times we just give up in frustration and discouragement. What's more, we feel constant confusion because we're unsure of how our eating habits relate to our Christian faith, if at all. We wonder about God's role in our lives and our response to Him. Where is He? What are His answers? It seems as though He should be able to help, but why isn't He answering our prayers? Why do we still struggle so?

Over the last ten years, I have agonized over these questions myself. I have also listened to hundreds of other women who were laboring to find answers to the same questions. As I have sought to minister to these women, I've learned that the Lord offers wonderful solutions to the problems of overeating, bulimia, and anorexia. I've written this book to share with you what I've learned on my journey from tyranny to freedom. It's my hope that you will find it helpful.

In the first ten chapters of this book we will look at the themes that are similar in each of these behaviors, and we'll discover practical guidelines for growth in godliness in our eating. In chapter eleven, we'll examine the areas that are distinctive to each behavior: anorexia, bulimia, and compulsive overeating. Chapter 12 offers some helpful encouragement, and finally, the section entitled *Practical Steps for Further Study* includes materials for personal application as well as questions for further study.

A Necessary Step

Before you begin to apply the principles in this book, you should visit your physician for a complete checkup so that you can be certain that the problems you are facing are not physiological in origin. Sometimes problems with eating and weight gain or loss are physical in origin. These problems may require medical attention. Don't assume that your problem is just an emotional or spiritual one. Prior to choosing any diet or exercise plan, you should have your doctor's consent. Also, if you are presently suffering from physical maladies because of obesity, bulimia, or anorexia, you will need to seek and follow your physician's advice. This book is not meant to take the place of any medical care that may be needed, but rather to augment it with spiritual and practical guidance.

A Sense of Purpose

Marsha began to grow in her relationship with God when she tried to answer the questions, "What am I doing here? What is the purpose of my life anyway?" She somehow sensed that her bouts of overeating and throwing up weren't part of what life was supposed to be about.

What about you? Do you believe that there is some purposeful design and meaning to your life, or do you feel you are just an evolved combination of molecules spinning aimlessly through a chaotic universe? For instance, is it just a coincidence that you happen to be here, now, reading this book? If you are a Christian, you *can* know that God does have a purpose for your life—and you can also be sure that His purpose is good. (If you aren't sure whether you're really a Christian or not, please take time now to read over "How to Really Know If You Are a Christian" at the end of this book.)

Marsha's questions aren't anything new. In fact, in the seventeenth century a group of Christians in England who were writing about their faith began by asking the question, "What is the chief end of man?" That was their way of asking, "What is our main purpose in life? Why are we here?" They answered by writing, "The chief end of man is to glorify God, and to enjoy Him forever."[1] Stop and reread that statement. Think about it. It's one of the most important truths that you will ever know. They believed that the primary purpose of life was twofold: First, they believed that you and I were put here principally to *bring glory* to God. I know that's kind of an astonishing thought—but, actually, that is the purpose of all of God's creation, isn't it? The mountains, the stars . . . why, the Bible says that even the trees "clap their hands" in giving glory to God. You can read about that in the Old Testament, in Isaiah 55:12. In the New Testament the apostle Paul puts the same thought this way: "Whether, then, you eat or drink or whatever you do, do all to the glory of God" (1 Corinthians 10:31).

Okay, you may be thinking, *everything is supposed to glorify God. But just what does that mean?* What that means is that everything we do—whether we're eating, drinking, reading a newspaper, driving our car, *whatever* we're doing—is to be done with the attitude and in such a way as to cause others around us to say, "Isn't God great! Isn't He wonderful! Isn't it great to know Him through His Son?"

Isn't that an astonishing thought? You and I can bring glory to God. It's not as though God needs us to let others know how great He is; it's because of His abounding grace and mercy that He has allowed us to be involved in this great plan and purpose.

Marsha was surprised to learn that God wanted to use her life—yes, even her eating habits—to show others that He was real and that He could change people. There are non-Christian members of my family who have seen how strong and good God is because they have seen that I have changed. My hope is that they will want to know more about God because they have seen my changed life. That's one way for me to "glorify" God.

The first step in learning to live a life that glorifies God is to realize that *every* part of our lives is lived *before Him*. You might think that God wants us to glorify Him only in those parts of our life that we might call "religious," such as going to church or praying or reading His Word. Or, it may seem that glorifying God is just for really spiritual people, like Billy Graham, or perhaps church leaders or pastors. But it's not just strong Christians who can glorify Him, nor is glorifying God limited to the spiritual realm. The Bible says we can look at *all* of our life as belonging to Him and as an avenue through which we can bless Him.

Remember, Paul said that we can glorify God whether we eat or drink or in *whatever* we do. What that meant to Marsha was that she could start thinking about ways to please God and point others to Him in every part of her life. Does God really care about how much we eat? Does He really care about whether or not we make ourselves throw up? Yes, God really cares. He cares because He loves you and me, and He cares because He created us to sparkle and shine with His light for others.

Let's return to the question, Why are we here? The Christians in England gave a two-part answer. They realized that we exist not only to glorify God, but also "to enjoy Him forever." God's plan is for you to *enjoy* Him! The same God who is the creator of the entire universe, who holds every-thing in its place by His power, who isn't bound by either time or space, also wants you to have such a close relationship with Him that you can say, "I really enjoy God. He satisfies my heart." The psalmist put it this way: "Whom have I in heaven but Thee? And besides Thee, I desire nothing on earth. My flesh and my heart may fail, but God is the strength of my heart and my portion forever" (Psalm 73:25-26). When you begin to get a picture of the sweetness, purity, and loveliness of the Lord, you will realize that all that the world has to offer is insignificant in comparison to Him.

Do you think about God in this way? Do you love worshiping Him? Spending time with Him? Thinking about Him? Do you want your entire life to be a song of worship and praise to Him? Do you find that He is your source of joy?

Angela had never thought of God as someone to enjoy. She knew that she should obey Him, but she didn't know anything of the delightfulness of His nature. To her, God was just a bunch of rules and regulations. She had missed the great wonder of His love and the sheer joy of spending time with Him. As she began to incorporate into her life the truths that she could glorify God and enjoy Him, she found that her tyrannical concern about how she looked began to fade in importance. Imagine being face to face with Jesus now. Imagine His kind voice, which always speaks the truth because He loves you more than anyone can imagine. Indeed, God loves His children, and you can have everlasting joy and peace because of it.

Today, God invites you to glorify and enjoy Him. He really is altogether lovely, isn't He? My hope is that what I've just shared helps to give you a right picture of God. He wants to use your life to glorify Himself and to bring you great joy. That is possible even for you. I know that because I've come to see that it is possible for every one of His children, including me, Marsha, and Angela.

Sit down. Kick your shoes off. Say, "Whew. God loves me and with His power, I can change." Won't you join me in receiving those truths in your heart . . . today?

2

THE CHANGE GOD DESIRES

"Beloved, now we are children of God,
and it has not appeared as yet what we shall be.
We know that, when He appears, we shall be like Him,
because we shall see Him just as He is."

—1 JOHN 3:2

I imagine that you wouldn't have picked up this book if you weren't interested in some sort of change in your life. Women frequently look for ways to improve and change their lives, but as a Christian, what kinds of changes should you seek?

This reminds me of a friend, Margaret, who was struggling with the very same question. "Elyse, I know it's absurd that I've spent my entire life thinking about how much I weigh and what I'm eating. And now that I'm a Christian, I've come to see that God wants more than this from me, but I just can't figure out what He wants me to do, or even how I should do it! Does God care how much I weigh? Just what *does* He want to do in my life?"

Margaret's confusion is understandable and common. A new Christian, her heart had changed and she now desired to please and love God, but her former habits of overeating and purging still controlled her. Margaret's questions are typical; confusion about God's perspective on eating and dieting is commonplace among many Christian women.

Does God really care how much you weigh or how you look? Does He want you to wear a certain dress size? Is He even concerned with such things? Does pleasing Him mean allowing Him to change your present image into something different?

Finding God's Answer

I myself have struggled to find the answers to those questions. I know that some Christians teach that God doesn't care about weight at all, while others say that desiring to look good is a God-given ambition—so He must care, right? How can I discern the difference between what God cares about and what is merely the thinking of our culture? One segment of our culture (Hollywood, the media, advertising) subtly proclaims that beauty is the foremost measurement of good, while another (primarily the feminist movement) teaches that outer beauty is completely insignificant. The church, as well, is confused. Should Christian women spend time trying to be the "Total Woman," get their "colors done," dress for success? Or should they shun makeup and contemporary hairstyles as mere trappings of the world? Are these issues just a matter of our own opinions, or is there a higher authority?

I believe that there is a place to discover God's thoughts about everything. It is in His Word, the Bible. That's what we read in the Old Testament: "Take to your heart all the words with which I am warning you today, which you shall command your sons to observe carefully, even all the words of this law. For it is not an idle word for you; *indeed it is your life*" (Deuteronomy 32:46-47). "Thy word is a lamp to my feet and a light to my path" (Psalm 119:105). There are also some verses in the New Testament that teach us God's purpose for Scripture: "These have been written that you may believe that Jesus is the Christ, the Son of God; and that believing *you may have life in His name*" (John 20:31, emphasis added); and 2 Peter 1:4: "He has granted to us His precious and magnificent promises, *in order that by them you might become partakers of the divine nature*, having escaped the corruption that is in the world by lust" (emphasis added). And finally, read what Paul wrote to Timothy about the purpose and power of the Bible:

> All Scripture is inspired by God and profitable for teaching, for reproof, for correction, for training in righteousness; that the man of God may be adequate, equipped for every good work (2 Timothy 3:16-17).

The Bible itself teaches that it is the *only* standard that can help us to know who God is and what He wants from us. You know, it doesn't really matter what anyone else thinks or says. It doesn't even matter what I think is right or what might sound good to me. What *He* says is what is important.

So, just what does God have to say to you about eating, dieting, and the desire to change?

The Reflection of Jesus in You

To begin with, I do believe that the Bible teaches that God is in the business of changing His children. But just what does this change look like? Is it primarily an outward transformation, or is it deeper and more comprehensive than just shrinking (or gaining) a few dress sizes? The change that God wants to accomplish in you is something much more meaningful, penetrating, and permanent than that. *He wants to change your heart so that you will become more and more like His Son, Jesus.* This is what Paul wrote to the church at Rome:

> We know that God causes all things to work
> together for good to those who love God, to those who
> are called according to His purpose. For whom He
> foreknew, He also predestined *to become conformed
> to the image of His Son*, that He might be the first-born
> among many brethren (Romans 8:28-29, emphasis
> added).

You know, God is making an amazing and very encouraging declaration of His plan for you here. Let's start at the beginning of this verse and think about what He's telling us.

What does God mean when He says that He "causes all things to work together for good"? For many years, I thought that these verses were simply a Band-Aid to be used when my washing machine overflowed or my child came home with a disappointing report card. In my heart I would say something like, "Well, I don't see any good in this, but God says it will all work out, so I guess it's okay." I don't say that to trivialize the daily trials you may face, but I now know that these verses are much more precious and profound than I ever realized. Read them again. He is causing everything that happens in your life—yes, *everything!*—to work toward the goal He has for you. What is that goal? For you "to become conformed to the image of His Son." *He wants you to be like His Son, Jesus Christ!* All the difficult circumstances you face—even your struggles with eating and your weight—are tools in the Master Sculptor's hand. He is using these tools to shape and mold you. Each trial, difficulty, joy, struggle, and tragedy is a precious instrument of His love! Even though being chiseled and hammered on all sides isn't comfortable, in His all-wise and loving hand, He's making you into a beautiful reflection of Himself. He's reaching out to you, changing you, filling you with a new inward holiness and grace. He wants you to be like a mirror that reflects the beauty of His Son.

Right away, you should recognize that this change is not primarily an outward one. It is essentially a change in the heart. The transformation that God wants to accomplish in you isn't merely the loss of 50 pounds or even the establishment of good eating habits. No, this transformation is much deeper than that. *He wants you to be like Jesus!* This is so astonishing! Think about it. God is so confident in His awesome power that as He sovereignly rules and overrules in your life, He *knows* He will accomplish the inconceivable task of recreating you to be like Christ.

He wants you to share in His confidence. He wants you to grasp the truth that He will accomplish His purpose in you. This is important because you are involved in a battle between faith and unbelief. When I look at my own life, the way that I consistently struggle with sin, I wonder if I will ever really change. I wonder if I will ever, in the innermost essence of who I am, be changed into His image. If all I had to look at was my own weak struggle, I too would be filled with unbelief. How can it be that He will change me? But I have something more than my own life to look at. I have Him. I have His Word. He tells me that He is working to accomplish His goal in my life, and even though everything in my experience wants to laugh (like Sarah in the Old Testament did) at His promise, I flee to faith in Him and in His astonishing power to transform. God wants us to have confidence in Him because without it, we would just give up in despair and discouragement. You can trust His Word.

When you face the reality of your present eating habits and the despair and hopelessness of never seeing any lasting change, take heart! If you are His child, then you can rest in the knowledge that "He does according to His will in the host of heaven and among the inhabitants of earth; and *no one* [not even you!] can ward off His hand" (Daniel 4:35, emphasis added). He will fulfill all His plans for you! Paul wrote:

> We should always give thanks to God for you, brethren beloved by the Lord, because *God has*

> *chosen you . . . for salvation through sanctifica-*
> *tion* [continual change] by the Spirit and faith
> in the truth (2 Thessalonians 2:13, emphasis
> added).

He's in the business of changing people. That includes you.

What God Calls "Good"

Just what does Paul mean when he writes that God causes "all things to work together for good"? Does he mean that God allows only pleasant things in our lives? We know by experience that this isn't the case. The washing machine does overflow. The kids do come home with disappointing report cards. We fail. In light of this, don't we need to ask ourselves, "Just how does God define 'good'?" I believe that Romans 8:29 shows us that God defines "good" as that which causes us to "become conformed to the image of His Son"—that which fulfills His plans for us. This definition of good is really a wonderful blessing when you stop and think about it. From God's perspective, He sees that this change in us is "good" because it causes us to be more like Him—the most wonderful, awesome Being in all of creation. And from our perspective, this change is "good" because it results in an abundance of overflowing joy and peace.

Does God want to change you? Yes, of course He does. Don't settle for some temporary outward change. Rest and rejoice in His promise to you. God has something better for His children; His change is eternal.

Developing Joyful Trust

Ginny wept quietly as she asked for prayer in our Bible study group. "I'm so tired of this 'character-building' . . . I just feel afraid and overwhelmed. I can't understand what God is doing. I want to submit to God's work in my life, but it's so hard. Where is He going with all this? Is this really necessary?"

Do you remember what we discovered in the previous chapter about God's purpose for us? We discovered that He desires to change our life so that we will "glorify Him and enjoy Him forever." You know, He wants to change us to become like Jesus for the same reason. He knows that the more like Jesus we become, the more we will glorify Him and enjoy His presence. For instance, I know that it's impossible to really enjoy the presence of a holy God if my life is filled with anxiety, fear, or self-indulgence. God wants me to be free from these things. And He wants the same thing for you, too. He wants to free you from your trust and dependence in yourself and give you the peace and joy that comes only when you are trusting in Him. Consider the words of Jeremiah the prophet:

> Blessed is the man who trusts in the LORD and whose trust is the LORD. For he will be like a tree planted by the water, that extends its roots by a stream and will not fear when the heat comes; but its leaves will be green, and it will not be anxious in a year of drought nor cease to yield fruit (Jeremiah 17:7-8).

Doesn't that sound delightful? There is a lake near my home and I very much enjoy walking around its banks. In one place, there is a stream that flows into it from the surrounding hills. The stream gurgles over rocks and is clear, clean, and cold. Its banks are lined with beautiful willows whose roots reach deeply into it for nourishment. Frequently, the path that takes me to this sweet haven is hot and dusty as the Southern California sun beats down upon it. What happy respite this shady stream brings after that dry, barren trail.

Now, reread Jeremiah 17:7-8, putting yourself in the verses. If you are trusting in Him, *you* are that lush tree whose roots are extending by the stream of God's grace and mercy. Even though the sun is beating down and it may even seem like a "year of drought," you can have the assurance that you won't wither. You have no need to anxiously look about you for help. You are rooted securely in Him. You will continue to produce the fruit He has ordained for you (Ephesians 2:10).

Trusting in Christ Alone

The only way to have a life that is like a lush tree by a river is to trust in God. It seems to me that my greatest struggle is learning to trust in Him. It's not that I don't trust Him for certain things—like my eternal home with Him; it's just that when it comes down to my everyday life, I frequently act as though I can handle difficult circumstances better than He can. It seems that I think that I am more wise or powerful than He is. I manipulate and grumble because I don't think that He's doing what He should for me. When I'm trusting in myself in this way, all I see is drought and difficulty.

Let me encourage you to put your whole trust in Him today. He wants to train your heart to glorify Him and enjoy Him forever. He wants to make you whole and holy. He wants to pour His peace and joy into your heart as you find your confidence in Him.

The word *trust* means more than just "believe." It means that you must put your confidence in Him; you must rely wholly upon Him. In the vernacular we might say, "Put all your eggs in one basket"—His basket. I might say that I trust such-and-such a thing will happen in the future. That's not the kind of trust I'm speaking of here. This kind of trust is a firm belief in the reliability of God. I must learn what He says about Himself—who He says He is—and then I must embrace this truth about Him. I can trust Him because I know His character—He's trustworthy!

Have you struggled with the whole matter of trusting God? Let's take a moment to look at some of His attributes so that we can be assured of the One in whom we are putting our confidence. God says that He is:

Eternal

God has no beginning, no end, and "in His existence there can be no succession of thoughts, feelings, or purposes. There can be no increase to His knowledge, no change to His purpose."[1] Psalm 33:11 says, "The counsel of the LORD stands forever, the plans of His heart from generation to generation." Psalm 90:2 tells us, "Before the mountains were born, or Thou didst give birth to the earth and the world, even from everlasting to everlasting, Thou art God."

You can rest in the truth that God fills all time. There has never been a time when He wasn't God. There won't ever come a day when we will have to mourn for His passing. He is the *living* God. This is a hard concept for us to grasp because all we know in our fleeting lives are beginnings and endings. Try to remember that for God there is no beginning or ending.

Immense

God fills all space. He "is simultaneously present every moment of time at every point of space."[2] "'Can a man hide himself in hiding places, so I do not see him?' declares the LORD. 'Do I not fill the heavens and the earth?' declares the LORD" (Jeremiah 23:24). In 1 Kings 8:27 we are asked, "Will God indeed dwell on the earth? Behold, heaven and the highest heaven cannot contain Thee. . . ." You can rely upon God because you will never be in a place where you are outside of the reach of His power and presence (Psalm 139:7-12).

Perfect in Holiness

Holiness is "on the one hand, entire freedom from moral evil and, on the other, absolute moral perfection."[3] In our God there are no wicked motives, no selfish schemes, no unjust actions. Think about 1 Samuel 2:2: "There is no one holy like the LORD, indeed, there is no one besides Thee, nor is there any rock like our God." Exodus 15:11 asks, "Who is like Thee among the gods, O LORD? Who is like Thee, majestic in holiness, awesome in praises, working wonders?" God is not holy because He has submitted to "some law or standard of moral excellence external to Himself, but [rather] all moral law and perfection have their eternal and unchangeable basis in His own nature."[4] God is perfectly holy, complete, whole, flawless, and pure. You can rely on Him because He is holy.

Perfect in Wisdom and Knowledge

God is infinite in His intelligence. This includes His omniscience (He knows everything) and His absolutely perfect wisdom. "Oh, the depth of the riches both of the wisdom and knowledge of God! How unsearchable are His judgments and unfathomable His ways! For who has known the mind of the Lord, or who became His counselor?" (Romans 11:33-34). Not only is God everywhere, at all times and in all space, but He also knows everything perfectly. Our perception is flawed; His is perfect. Unlike you and me, He understands all things as they really are—He never misunderstands. In addition, His wisdom is perfect. He decides both the means and the ends to accomplish all of His perfect plans. You can trust Him because our Father *really does* know best.

Filled with Goodness

This goodness includes God's benevolence, love, mercy, and grace. His goodness is shown in His disposition to promote the happiness of His miserable, weak, and undeserving children. "Every good thing bestowed and every perfect gift is from above, coming down from the Father of lights, with whom there is no variation, or shifting shadow"

(James 1:17). Look at how Exodus 34:6-7 describes God: "Then the LORD passed by in front of him and proclaimed, 'The LORD, the LORD God, compassionate and gracious, slow to anger, and abounding in lovingkindness and truth; who keeps lovingkindness for thousands, who forgives iniquity, transgression and sin.'"

If you are God's child, you don't ever have to doubt God's goodness toward you. He wants to secure your eternal happiness. When I say that God "wants to secure your eternal happiness," you need to understand what I mean. I mean that He wants to teach you that eternal happiness will be found *only* in Him because He alone is the fountain of true joy. When your heart is centered on Him, rejoicing in His character and goodness, you will be truly happy. It is because He is good and knows that your happiness will be made full only in Him that He is teaching you to center your life in Him. That is why Paul wrote, "set your mind on the things above, and not on the things that are on earth" (Colossians 3:1). Our hearts inherently take more delight in the creation (what we experience with our senses) rather than the Creator, and God uses His Word and circumstances to free us from our love of the world. It is because of this worldly love that your eternal happiness and your temporal happiness are frequently at odds. Because He is good, your temporal happiness is not God's ultimate goal. He knows that if you are to be eternally happy, your earthly happiness may need to be sacrificed for a time—perhaps even a lifetime. Remember that God's ultimate goal is that He be glorified, and this is accomplished partly by filling you with joy and praise in Him, and partly by changing you to be like Him. On the other hand, when your circumstances are difficult, it's not that God is looking for ways to make you miserable. It's just that He knows what will make you happy in the end, and it's toward that goal that He is continually working.[5] He is truly filled with goodness. He's making you fit for heaven and His presence. "Most men hope to go to heaven when they die, but few, it may be feared, take the trouble to consider whether they would enjoy heaven if they got there. . . . to be really happy in heaven, it is clear and plain that we must be somewhat trained and made ready for heaven while we are on earth."[6] That's what God, in His goodness, is doing—making you fit for heaven and filling your heart with praise for Him now.

Filled with Truth

We live in a time when it seems as though we have lost the concept of truth. God's truth is *always* true. It isn't just true today for me or for certain people. Some people say, "Well, if you have found your own truth, that's great . . . I just don't think it's true for me." However, God's communication with us is always true, correct, valid, and dependable.

Have you ever been fooled by someone or something? Remember that God can neither be deceived nor deceive. "Thy lovingkindness is great to the heavens, and Thy truth to the clouds" (Psalm 57:10). "Thou, O Lord, art a God merciful and gracious, slow to anger and abundant in lovingkindness and truth" (Psalm 86:15). You can trust God because He never lies: "God is not a man, that He should lie . . . has He said, and will He not do it? Or has He spoken, and will He not make it good?" (Numbers 23:19).

You may remember the Christian bumper sticker some years ago that read, "God said it, I believe it, that settles it." I can understand what the author of the bumper sticker meant, but it really should say, "God said it; that settles it." God's truth doesn't change just because I might not believe it. It is always truth. You can trust God because His Word is always true.

Look back over the brief list of God's characteristics. Which ones are the most meaningful to you? Which ones are difficult for you to understand? Why not ask the Lord to open your understanding to His awesome character now so that you will grow to trust Him more? Remember the picture of the lush green tree by the river. That's you under

His care. He will help you grow and change you into a beautiful, flourishing tree, reflecting His glory. Put your whole trust in Him today. We'll talk more later about what trusting Him means, but let's just suffice it to say that it involves resting in Him, believing what He says, and following His directions in every part of your life.

The Benefit of Change

You've learned that God wants to change you so that you will consistently reflect His character to the world. One of the benefits of being changed into His likeness is the joy that comes from communing with Him regularly. Consider this verse from the Psalms: "Thou wilt make known to me the path of life; in Thy presence is fulness of joy; in Thy right hand there are pleasures forever" (Psalm 16:11). There is such joy and pleasure in God's presence! The more like Him you become, the more you will love to celebrate His fellowship with you.

So, back to the question at hand: Is God interested in changing you? Yes, of course He is. But that change is initially an inward one. I'm not saying that you shouldn't think about losing weight if you're overweight, or gaining weight if you're too thin. I'm just saying that is the wrong focus. Your focus should be on pleasing your heavenly Father with a heart that is fully trusting, fully resting, fully rejoicing in His love.

3

MIRROR, MIRROR, IN MY HEART

"The King's daughter is all glorious within;
her clothing is interwoven with gold."

—PSALM 45:13

Lisa and I had been working together on her habitual anorexia for a few weeks. After looking over her menu from the week before, on which she indicated that she had not eaten more than 200 calories on any of the days, I asked her why she was continuing to starve herself. This was her answer: "If I start eating, I might gain weight!"

"Yes, and then what would happen?" I asked.

"I wouldn't look good!" she replied.

"And then what?"

"I don't know, but it scares me to death!" exclaimed Lisa. "What would happen to me if I gained weight? What if I ended up looking like my mom? I can't imagine myself looking like that."

"Do you care about what others think of how you look?" I asked.

"No, it's nothing like that. It's me. I just can't stand the thought of becoming fat!"

The "Beautiful People"

Our culture today has influenced many women to see themselves solely in the context of how they look. We are continuously bombarded by image after image of seemingly perfect women with perfect teeth, perfect hair, perfect figures.[1] And because we live in a time when we are connected technologically with the entire world, we are not merely competing with one or two women from our own village. We feel that we are compelled to compete with the most beautiful women in the entire world!

Why are so many women driven to compete with one another in this way? Why would Lisa starve herself and then exercise to the point of collapse? Why do thousands of men and women spend billions of dollars every year just to *look good?*

Believing the Lie[2]

It seems to me that we act this way because we're willing to believe a lie. Here is what I believe the lie is: *It is that somehow, if we could just look like the latest supermodel, we would find true happiness and contentment.* We would have peace and joy. We would have the adoration of others. We would no longer have to worry about paying bills or staying up with sick children. Life would be perfect. We are deceived into thinking that being beautiful is the answer to all of our problems.

Jean, a thin woman who didn't have any significant problems with eating habits, was in one of my Bible study classes with other women who were struggling with their weight. She looked shocked when I asked her one evening if she thought that being thin meant that she could serve or please God with greater ease. I asked her if she believed that her life was easier because she wasn't always fighting her weight. "Of course not! I struggle with all of the same things that you struggle with, but just in different areas. My life isn't any better because I'm not overweight." The other women (most of whom were overweight) were surprised.

Our world's obsession with outward appearance and weight has led many of us to think in shallow terms about what makes for peace and joy. "If I could just wear a size 8 (or if my hips weren't so big, or if I had a smaller waist, or . . .), I know I would be content, successful, or happy." As silly as that sounds, I know that many women subconsciously think that way. I confess that I have thought that way. (As if there isn't an unhappy size 8 woman anywhere in the world!) We believe the lie that outward perfection (which, by the way, is an impossible goal) is the key to inner peace and joy. Or perhaps we are duped into thinking that the false happiness and contentment that comes from being satisfied with the image we see in the mirror is the true peace and contentment that we are seeking from our relationship with God. We seek after lesser joys.

Surface Blemishes

Why would we be willing to believe such a ridiculous lie? Aside from the fact that the cultural pressures to "look good" are enormous (particularly in Southern California, where I live), isn't there something inherently attractive in thinking that our problems are only skin deep? Don't we want to believe that the difficulties we face in life are really just because our ankles are too large or our breasts are too small? "No," I reassure my accusing heart, "I don't have a sin problem . . . I'm not a rebel or an idolater. I just have this little appearance problem. It's really no big deal and once I lose 50 pounds (or gain 15 pounds, or get in shape, or have that cosmetic surgery, or . . .), then my life will really be just fine, thank you." This focus on outward appearance is a nifty distraction from my real character defects. The apostle

John speaks forcefully about the source of this thinking in 1 John 2:16: "All that is in the world, the lust of the flesh and the lust of the eyes and the boastful pride of life, is not from the Father, but is from the world."

All you need to do is watch a few moments of television to know that this is the lie that has duped our generation. "Buy these jeans and you'll be popular!" "Drink this beer and women will love you!" "Attend these diet classes and you'll be able to rejoice in your new size and dance in front of the mirror! Don't wait any longer . . . because, after all, you're worth it!" We must strive to put aside the thinking that's so common in our culture.

Biblical counselor David Powlison writes powerfully about this kind of thinking:

> What happens when someone embraces such values? They live out the logic of their faith in countless ways. Perhaps, most commonly, many women feel an abiding, low-grade anxiety about their appearance. It might manifest as subtly as spending an unnecessary extra couple of minutes in front of the mirror trying to fix what is unacceptable . . . or stewing internally in regrets and "if onlys." Mental or actual tinkering with appearance can chew up amazing amounts of time and energy. Or perhaps upon walking into the fellowship hall after church, a woman is instantly aware of what every other woman is wearing, and has sized up how she compares. Her very gaze at other people is conditioned to a status hierarchy defined by images of beauty, and thus to the attendant jealousy, self-loathing, competitiveness, inferiority/superiority comparisons, and the like. Perhaps she obsessively pursues alterations in her appearance: hair color, weight loss, new clothing, makeup, cosmetic operations. Perhaps she slides into an "eating disorder." Perhaps she plunges into despair and gives up, gaining 100 pounds, becoming unkempt, "uglify-

ing" herself. "I'm a failure" simply registers a different manifestation of devotion to the lie. All such preoccupations rob her of the joy and freedom of faith in Christ the Lord, and sap energies that might be spent in loving concern for others.[3]

If we just stopped to think logically, we would know that pursuing this lie is futile and pointless. I know from personal experience that as long as my heart is focused on "looking good," there will never be a time when I am completely satisfied with my appearance. I will never find the peace and joy that I am seeking in the mirror because my heart will always want more and more. God didn't create me to find joy in my reflection in the mirror. Because I'd be living contrary to God's truth, I'd never find satisfaction in that pursuit. As in the case of the evil queen in *Snow White*, the mirror will always tell me that there is someone in the realm fairer than I. That would only fill me with anxiety, jealousy, or despair, and cause me to refocus my efforts . . . just 5 more pounds . . . just a different type of makeup . . . just these new shoes or earrings or perfume . . . just one bite from this poisoned apple, and all my problems will be solved.

Sometimes, in frustration and discouragement, I give up. "I'll never be as pretty as so-and-so. I'll never lose weight. I'll just give up and have something to eat! If I can't look good, I'll at least have the pleasure of this food." This focus is so futile, so hopeless, so frustrating. Why persist in it? How much time, effort, and money must be sacrificed to the god in the mirror before we finally realize that we're chasing the wind?

Is It Wrong to Look Good?

Judith was growing more and more in her understanding of Christ and her sanctification. In one of our studies, after a discussion about proper motives, she said, "But, I really want to look good. There isn't anything wrong with that, is there?" I had to stop and think. Is there anything wrong with wanting to look good? What does the Bible say about outward appearance? Immediately I remembered Proverbs 31:30: "Charm is deceitful and beauty is vain, but a woman who fears the LORD, she shall be praised."

What is God teaching women here? First, He says that charm or grace of manner is a "mere semblance, an outward varnish."[4] Like the varnish that you might paint over a piece of wood, worldly charm doesn't involve the heart—its only concern is appearances. *How do I look?* I wonder. *Am I sufficiently covering myself up so that you think that I am beautiful, chic, sophisticated, unconcerned about your opinion?*

Second, Proverbs 31:30 teaches that beauty is vain, futile; it is so fleeting. How many years can a woman look good—30, maybe 40? Even a woman as beautiful as Elizabeth Taylor must, in the end, acquiesce to time. The debutante of National Velvet has aged, and all of the cosmetics and surgeries in the world can't stop the march of time. Our beauty, such as it is, will always be marred by age or illness. It will perish. First Peter 3:3-4 says, "Let not your adornment be merely external—braiding the hair, and wearing gold jewelry, or putting on dresses; but let it be the hidden person of the heart, with the *imperishable quality of a gentle and quiet spirit,* which is precious in the sight of God" (emphasis added). Our outer beauty will perish, but the inner qualities that God cherishes won't. "You will also be a crown of beauty in the hand of the LORD, and a royal diadem in the hand of your God" (Isaiah 62:3).

Please don't misunderstand me. I am not saying that a woman should be completely oblivious to the way that she looks. Nor am I saying that it is either godly or ungodly to "wear makeup or try to look good by exercising, buying clothes (as you can afford to), or learning new ways to fix your hair. I'm not called to judge anyone else's spirituality by the outer body. . . ."[5]

Our culture highly values outward appearance and although we must not worship our own image in the mirror, I don't believe that it is sinful to seek to look presentable, *per se*. The issue is really one of obedience and trust. Are you seeking to be obedient in your use of your time, your financial resources? If you are spending much of your time consumed with thoughts about how you look or standing in front of the mirror trying to fix that bothersome problem, you should question whether your concerns about your appearance are a higher priority than they should be. Are you spending a large percentage of your finances on your hair, your clothing, your makeup, your nails, your gym dues? Do you put yourself in debt in your pursuit of beauty? Are you trusting in the way that you look to enable you to experience peace and joy, to control your world, to garner praise for yourself?

These are the questions you must ask yourself, and no one but you can draw the line between what is appropriate and what is sinful. If you are focused on loving Christ and want to wear makeup, dye your hair, dress with pizzaz, go for it! If, on the other hand, you're filled with the desire for the praise of others, you need to learn to seek to please the Lord instead. This means that you might put a limit on your expenditures of time and money, or seek to minister to others in situations where you would normally desire that people give you compliments.

Trying to Avoid the Inevitable

Among unbelievers and particularly those who set the styles, is this worship of youth and beauty just one more reaction against the inevitability of death? The truth is that those who don't know Christ are charging full-speed ahead, to a terrifying and inevitable end. Could it be that this worship of youth and beauty is a welcome deception as they seek to forestall the inevitable for as long as possible, fooling themselves into believing that they are immortal—that they are always young?

The Christian, however, should have a different perspective. Death is not to be feared. It is to be welcomed because its sting—fear of the punishment of eternal separation from God because of judgment for sin—has been removed. In fact, Paul teaches that in death this body of ours, this old tent, will be torn down and clothed with life. He says in 2 Corinthians 5, "We know that if the earthly tent which is our house is torn down, we have a building from God, a house not made with hands, eternal in the heavens. . . . For indeed while we are in this tent, we groan, being burdened, because we do not want to be unclothed, but to be clothed, *in order that what is mortal may be swallowed up by life*" (verses 1,4). We long "to leave this body that we may go to Christ, and to put off these *rags of mortality* that we may put on the *robes of glory*"[6] (emphasis added). Only then, as we shine with His perfect life, will we know true, lasting beauty reflecting the glory of the King of heaven.

Living in Southern California, I love to watch the sunset over the Pacific Ocean. Sometimes when it appears that there might be an especially nice sunset, my husband will drive me down to the beach in the late afternoon. We'll sit on the grass for an hour or so and observe God's handiwork in motion. I've found that a few clouds make for the most beautiful sunsets. As the sun sinks down on the horizon, it shoots out golden beams of light that make the clouds look iridescent. The effect is spellbinding as scarlet, amber, pink, lavender, and golden skies shine down on a sparkling blue-green sea. Sometimes it just takes my breath away. When I see these spectacular displays, I am reminded that this earth (as magnificent as it sometimes may be) is only a vague shadow of the beauty of heaven. How beyond expression must the grandeur and excellence of heaven be! *We will be clothed with life straight from God's throne!* We will shine with more beauty than the most exquisite sunset! Are we seeking to prepare ourselves for God's dressing room, or are we consumed with the meager rags of this earth?

No Biblical Command to Be Thin

Now, I'm going to say something that may seem rather surprising. You know, I've read the Bible straight through many times, and *I've never found any Scripture that commands or even commends thinness!* Think of that. I don't believe that there is any verse in either the Old or New Testament that encourages Christians to be thin or states that being thin is a mark of godliness. Keeping in mind the fact that God's Word, the Bible, is our guide for life, it appears that many of us (including me) have spent much of our lives chasing after something that God doesn't seem to think is very important.

Now, before you throw this book down in frustration and run to the bookstore for a new book on dieting, please understand what I'm saying. Just because God doesn't command thinness doesn't mean that we should ignore our health or our eating habits. If that were the case, this book would be over now and I would just encourage you to go out and eat, drink, and be merry. While there *are* some biblical concerns that can be brought to bear on our health and eating habits—such as learning to desire only Him, thinking about your life the way that He does, and learning to discern whether your eating habits are godly— the whole matter of "thinness for thinness' sake" isn't one of them.

Seeking after thinness merely for appearance's sake is not a godly goal. That's because it falls into the categories that we have already been discussing—such as the pursuit of outward beauty (what the Bible calls vanity) and all of its attending futility.

An Eternal Makeover

The kind of beauty that God desires for you is found in 1 Peter 3:4: ". . . the imperishable quality of a gentle and quiet spirit." It is called the "fruit of the Spirit" (the results of the Holy Spirit's work in your life) in Galatians 5:22-23: "love, joy, peace, patience, kindness, goodness, faithfulness, gentleness, self-control." The excellent woman in Proverbs 31 is known for her industry, wisdom, strength, confidence, generosity, courage, knowledge, optimism, and kindness. Since we've already looked at the beginning of verse 30, let's see the way the verse ends: "Charm is deceitful and beauty is vain, but a woman who fears the LORD, she shall be praised." The fear of the Lord is a defining characteristic of a godly woman. A woman who fears the Lord will be growing in all of the qualities listed above. But what does it mean to "fear" God?

One Bible dictionary defines the function of godly fear in this way: It has the meaning of "standing in awe. This is not simple fear, but reverence, whereby an individual recognizes the power and position of the individual revered and renders him proper respect. . . . There is more involved here than mere psychological fear."[7] Godly fear involves proper honor and reverence.

A Fear to Be Desired

Charles Spurgeon taught the true meaning of this concept when he preached in London more than 100 years ago:

> Blessed is the man whose heart is filled with that holy fear which inclines his steps in the way of God's commandments, inclines his heart to seek after God, and inclines his whole soul to enter into fellowship with God, that he may be acquainted with Him, and be at peace. What is this fear of God? I answer, first, it is a *sense of awe of His greatness*.

Have you never felt this sacred awe stealing insensibly over your spirit, hushing, and calming you, and bowing you down before the Lord? It will come, sometimes, in the consideration of the great works of nature. Gazing upon the vast expanse of waters—looking up to the innumerable stars, examining the wing of an insect, and seeing there the matchless skill of God displayed in the minute; or standing in a thunderstorm, watching, as best you can, the flashes of lightning, and listening to the thunder of Jehovah's voice, have you not often shrunk into yourself, and said, "Great God, how terrible art Thou!"—*not afraid, but full of delight like a child* who rejoices to see his father's wealth, his father's wisdom, his father's power—happy, and at home, but feeling oh, so little! We are less than nothing, we are all but annihilated in the presence of the great eternal, infinite, invisible All-in-all (emphasis added).[8]

Seeking His Kingdom

Each concept that we have been talking about in this chapter is summed up in the phrase, "Fear God." Instead of believing the lies from the world—lies that tell you that outer beauty is the road to happiness—you should learn to fear God and believe what He says about you. Let His Word tell you what you should value, what you should seek after, what you should fear. Instead of fearing other's opinions about you, how you look, and your value, you should fear and seek God, your wonderful heavenly Father.

Remember what the Lord Jesus taught: "Seek first His kingdom and His righteousness . . ." (Matthew 6:33). Then, let that encouragement spur you on to the pursuit of the inner, godly characteristics that He desires for you. Remember that He is in the process of changing you—a process that will find its completion when you are beautifully robed in His glory in heaven. Don't settle for a mere 15-pound weight loss or even the good but temporary establishment of healthy eating habits. Submit yourself to His work in your life—rejoice in it like a "child who rejoices to see his father's wealth, his father's wisdom, his father's power"!

PART TWO

~

Understanding Who You Are

4

WE ARE GOD'S TEMPLE

*"We are His workmanship, created in Christ Jesus
for good works...."*

—EPHESIANS 2:10

We have already spent a good deal of time discussing the reasons we shouldn't be concerned with our outward appearance. We have talked about the real reason for our life, which is to glorify God and enjoy Him forever. We've learned about God's standards, which are found in His Word, the Bible. We've talked about God's desire to change us into the image or likeness of His Son. We've discussed the lie that the world propagates—the lie that says that the pathway to peace and joy is through outward beauty. We've learned that the Bible does not command or commend thinness for thinness' sake, and that seeking after a beautiful body is not God's will for our life. We've been encouraged to fear God instead of what others think and to seek Him exclusively. Now we're ready to move on and gain further understanding about caring for our bodies.

You might be wondering why, after all this, I've written a book about proper eating habits. It would seem odd, after everything I've just said, that I'm now going to encourage you to think very carefully about your eating and your diet. If, after all, these things aren't all that important, and if the Bible doesn't speak about thinness, then why be concerned about it?

You should be concerned about caring for your body for two reasons: first, because it is the creation of God. And second, if you are a Christian, God purchased your body. Let's take a closer look at the first of these two reasons.

Fearfully and Wonderfully Made

Consider these precious words from Psalm 139:13-14: "Thou didst form my inward parts; Thou didst weave me in my mother's womb. I will give thanks to Thee, for I am fearfully and wonderfully made; wonderful are Thy works, and my soul knows it very well."

I have to be honest: When I read these verses about my body being fearfully and wonderfully made, sometimes I have a hard time believing it. I know that frequently I'm not thankful the way that I should be. I wonder why my body isn't the way that *I* want it to be. I wonder why I have friends who can eat whatever they want and remain thin. I wonder why my arms, no matter how many push-ups I might do, continue to look like my grandmother's. I wonder why I have to continuously struggle with "the battle of the bulge." Why is my body the way it is? Why did God create me the way that I am? I have to be careful when I begin to think this way—that I don't blame God for my own sin (overeating or laziness about exercise). But on the other hand, I do have a predisposition to look a certain way. That is how I was created.

Perhaps you can relate to what I'm saying. Do you wish you were shorter or taller? Do you wish that you didn't have the metabolism that you have? Perhaps you have a genetic problem or handicap. Perhaps you don't like your freckles or your skin that burns too easily or the curliness or lack of curls in your hair. Perhaps you think that if you could just be like so-and-so, you know you could be thankful because then you would know that you were "fearfully and wonderfully made."

My body reminds me of my paternal grandmother's. I have childhood memories of sitting on her lap—it was very soft and I could sink into it. My brother and I would play with my grandmother's arms. Yes, they were arms that you could actually play with! In Billy Crystal's movie *Mr. Saturday Night*, he describes his mother's arms as being those of the "Jewish Batwoman." I laughed hysterically when I first heard him say this, because I knew just what he meant. I have fond memories of my grandmother's arms. However, I don't think that I've been very thankful that I inherited them. If the decision was mine to make, I would rather have inherited something else from her.

Let's take a moment to think about what God is saying to us when He encourages us to be thankful because we are "fearfully and wonderfully made." In Psalm 139, where those words appear, the writer first rejoices in the knowledge of God's omniscience (He's all-knowing) and omnipresence (He's present everywhere). He rejoices that God knows every thought he has, and, yes, the Lord even knows the words he will say before he says them. He basks in the security of God's presence. He knows that no matter where he goes, whether up into the heavens, down into hell, into the depths of the sea, or even into complete darkness, he cannot go out of the view of God's watchful eye or the grasp of His loving hand. He's amazed because he knows that God's thoughts are toward him even when he sleeps! "How precious," he writes, "also are Thy thoughts to me, O God! How vast is the sum of them! If I should count them, they would outnumber the sand. When I awake, I am still with Thee."

Next, the writer turns his gaze inward. He recognizes that every detail about the way his body was created was an act of God's loving care. He thanks God that He was conscious of his life even before his life had true consciousness. God was actively involved with him while he was being "knit together" in his mother's womb. Yes, even then, before his own self-consciousness, in the darkness of his mother's body, God was there. God was overseeing and ruling in the forming of his body. He was creating him uniquely, granting him the strengths and the gifts and blessing him with the imperfections and the weaknesses that would best glorify Himself and make for His child's eternal happiness. Do you think that the writer of this psalm was free from any physical defects? Since no one is, we are forced to recognize that *our thankfulness for God's creation comes from a heart that delights in His work, not in our appraisal of it.* God created *you* to be the way that you are.

Psalm 139 is a psalm of great assurance and confidence. Nothing in all of your life, including your body, is beyond God's care, power, and sovereign rule. No matter what trial I'm facing—whether it's coming to me from the outside, perhaps in some form of persecution or difficulty, or it's coming to me from within—I'm not alone. God isn't surprised; He isn't unaware.

Stop and consider the greatness of God's creation in your body. Even though you might have certain predispositions or conditions, still, God has exalted you by giving you a body that is the most intricate and blessed of all His creation. Think about the wonder of a cell, of your eyesight, your ability to process information and make decisions. God has set humankind apart from all of His creation as being made in His own image. We reflect His character in many ways. Our intelligence, volition, and emotions all reflect—though dimly—His greatness.

God has also made the human body frail. He has done so in order that we might learn to depend upon Him. It is wise to think that the physical problems that we face are each one precious gifts given to us. He gives them to us so that we will continuously rely upon Him as our strength. I thank God that I wasn't given the body that I have desired because then I wouldn't care about helping others who struggle like I do. Perhaps I would be even more vain than I am. Perhaps I would look down on others and not have compassion for their plight. Yes, I can thank God because He has made me the way that I am. I can thank God because He's accomplishing His goal of glorifying Himself and changing me through the problems I face with my body. I won't lie to you and say that I always enjoy these trials. It's just that I know that when I think about God—His love, grace, and mercy in Christ—I can rejoice. Everything that He has made is very good.

Your body is God's creation. Because of this, you should care for it because you love Him and want to honor Him. You should eat properly because you want to show Him that you are thankful for His wondrous works. You should care for your body because you want to demonstrate to the world that there is a Creator and that life, even your life, must be attended to because it flows from Him. Contrary to modern Darwinian thought, you are not just a bunch of randomly developed molecules that happened to form up from a creature that emerged from some slime pit millions of years ago. No, your body is the distinctive creation of God. Because of this, you should care for your body and seek to develop a heart of thankfulness for both your strengths and weaknesses.

Caretakers in God's Home

We have already examined the first of two biblical reasons why we should be concerned about proper eating habits: We are the unique creation of God. The second reason is that, if we are Christians, *our bodies belong to God as His sanctuary*. God did not create us and then wander off to see about something else. No . . . if we are His child, He lives within us! Let's consider what the following passages from 1 Corinthians has to say about the body:

Do you not know that your body is a temple of the Holy Spirit who is in you, whom you have from

God, and that you are not your own? For you have
been bought with a price: therefore glorify God in
your body (1 Corinthians 6:19-20).

Do you not know that you are a temple of God,
and that the Spirit of God dwells in you? . . . for the
temple of God is holy, and that is what you are
(1 Corinthians 3:16-17).

What is Paul teaching here? First, he is teaching that if
you are a Christian, your physical body is the dwelling
place or sanctuary of God's Spirit. The word used here for
"temple" is the very same word that is used to describe the
temple building that was in Jerusalem. Today, instead of
dwelling in a physical building, God dwells in those of us
who are Christians—both as individuals and as members
of the body of Christ, the church. Just as the presence of
God dwelt in His temple in Old Testament times, so the Holy
Spirit lives in you today. Just as that temple was conse-
crated, set apart, possessed, occupied, and inhabited by
God, so now you are His temple, a place where He dwells
. . . and your body is to be sacred to His use. Your body is
set apart, occupied, and inhabited by God. For you to act
otherwise would be contradictory. That's why you are
called to keep your body holy for Him. Just as you would
not walk into a church building and desecrate it, so you are
to keep your body holy because it's God's home.

Just think of it: *The God who created the entire universe
and whose presence fills that universe is pleased to live, by
His Spirit, in you!* One writer put it this way:

Your body is the temple of the Holy Spirit! What
an astonishing saying is this! As truly as the living
God dwelt in the Mosaic tabernacle, and in the
temple of Solomon, so truly does the Holy Spirit
dwell in the souls of genuine Christians; and as the
temple and all its utensils were holy, separated from
all common and profane uses, and dedicated alone

to the service of God, so the bodies of genuine
Christians are holy, and all their members should
be employed in the service of God alone.[1]

Look at the way that Jesus describes this indwelling: "If
anyone loves Me, he will keep My word; and My Father will
love him, and We will come to him, *and make Our abode
with him*" (John 14:23, emphasis added). You know, one of
Jesus' names in the Bible is "Immanuel"—that name
means, "God with us." Part of one of the blessings of heaven
is that God will be with us in a very concrete way, according to the Bible's description of heaven in the book of
Revelation: "I heard a loud voice from the throne, saying,
'Behold, the tabernacle of God is among men, and He shall
dwell among them, and they shall be His people, and God
Himself shall be among them'" (Revelation 21:3). The
wonderful joy of heaven lies in the reality of God's unre-
strained presence with us.

Because your body is God's temple, you should treat it
with care and concern. This means many things—not just
that you should eat properly. It means that you should be
careful to get enough rest and exercise. You should learn
how to handle stressful situations in a way that doesn't
cause harm to your body. For as long as God gives you
health, and in whatever way He does so, you should thankfully seek to be a good steward or manager of what He's
given.

Shelley, a friend of mine who is diabetic, had to learn
this lesson the hard way. She frequently found herself at the
doctor's office and sometimes even at the hospital because
she thought that she was too busy to be bothered with the
routine that her physician has prescribed. I could tell that
this routine was difficult, time consuming, and painful, and
Shelley really chafed under this regimen. Yet my friend
matured in her walk with Christ when she realized that her
body did not belong to her, but was instead the home of the
Lord she loved. She submitted herself to all of the daily

inconveniences, the blood tests, the shots, and the meticulous diet so that she could preserve her body for His use. Although these practices were disagreeable to her, she understood that God wanted to use her (and her body) in His service so that she could accomplish the work He had given her. Thus she began to make a real effort at caring for herself. She wanted God to be able to use her illness for His glory. She glorified Him in her illness by thankfully and carefully submitting to His plan for her life and taught her children how to rejoice in God's goodness, even in the middle of adversities.

Many of us have chronic maladies that seem to limit our ability to serve God unrestrictedly. Some of these illnesses come because we live in a world that has been infected with sin and death. Disease and death are part of our daily lives. While there are some illnesses we cannot avoid, there are others that we bring upon ourselves because we have destroyed our health through unwise practices. As I talk about the importance of caring for our bodies, I'm not teaching that God has promised absolute health to any of us (at least not while we're here in this earthly body). Rather, I am teaching that we have a responsibility to care for the body that God has given us and to maintain as good health as possible. We are not to focus on good health as a god, nor are we to think that by following a super-fastidious diet we can shake off God's hand if it's time for us to die. We are, however, to be careful that we are not doing anything that would purposely destroy or desecrate the body—remember, it's God's temple that we have been given. Your body is one of God's tools in the world. Care for it as you would care for a beautiful sanctuary.

Are you focusing on perfecting your body or health as some pathway to peace and joy? Or have you turned your focus on God's presence in you and His need of your faithful service? If you are weak from self-starvation, if your esophagus is eroded from vomiting, if you are so overweight that your heart and muscles cannot function properly, then your usefulness to the Lord may be hindered or cut short in some ways.

The Sixth Commandment and You

The sixth commandment is, "Thou shalt not kill" (Exodus 20:13 KJV). I would imagine that the thought of actually murdering someone is far from most of us. We mourn when we hear about shootings at schools. We observe National Right to Life Day in remembrance of the millions of infants who have been aborted in our nation over the last 30 years. We are troubled over the rising murder rates in many of our cities. This is as it should be. But, is it possible that we could be guilty of a kind of murder ourselves by the way that we treat our bodies?

According to the Westminster Larger Catechism, some of the duties required by the sixth commandment include the following: "*to preserve the life of ourselves* and others by resisting all thoughts and purposes, subduing all passions, and avoiding all occasions, temptations, and practices, which tend to the unjust taking away of life of any . . . *a sober use of meat, drink . . . sleep, labor, and recreations. . . .*"[2] I know that the way those words are written is antiquated. We hardly speak of a "sober" use of meat or drink anymore. But I think there is real truth here. In more modern terms, the writers of this catechism believed that the sixth commandment taught not only that we must protect other's lives, but that we also had an obligation to protect our own life. We must be careful to avoid overeating or starvation, drunkenness, and overwork. We must moderate our recreations so that we do not ruin our health by them, and we must not work so hard that we neglect God's command to preserve our life through Sabbath rest. Wherever you are in your lifespan—whether you are a young woman, full of strength and vitality, or a middle-aged woman feeling strong and yet recognizing that youth has passed, or an older woman struggling with declining health—you must look at the body you now have as a precious gift from your Lord to care for.

You probably won't have perfect health all of your life. Most people don't. But, as long as you do have life, you should do your best to protect it. If that means remembering to take your medication or rest, if that means building an exercise regimen into your sedentary lifestyle, if that means learning how to cheerfully embrace life under God's sovereign rule and love and stop worrying, then begin to do so now. *Just remember that caring for your body is not the goal of life—glorifying and loving God is.* Caring for your body is merely a means to an end and one way to say thank you to the Lord for all of the things He has done for you.

Restoring the Years of Loss

I hope that these thoughts don't discourage you or bring you any sense of condemnation. Perhaps you've never thought about your body in this way before, and now it seems as though it's almost too late. Perhaps you are already suffering the effects of neglecting or abusing your body. Don't give up. It's never too late to begin serving God. He can restore and help you. Listen to these words from the prophet Joel: "I will make up to you for the years that the swarming locust has eaten, the creeping locust, the stripping locust, and the gnawing locust, My great army which I sent among you" (Joel 2:25). God's people had sinned and they were reaping the consequences of their behavior. Just think—God could have said, "Well, tough luck, guys. I told you not to sin and you went ahead, so now you'll just have to reap the consequences of your actions." But that's not what He does. No, He calls them to repentance, and then He tells them that He will make up for all the losses they have suffered.

Today you may be suffering from diabetes, weakened joints, or heart problems caused by your overeating; you may be suffering with an eroded esophagus or swollen glands or even an inability to keep any food down; perhaps you've starved yourself and your bones and skin are weak and your heart has been damaged. Don't despair—God can still use and fill you. Perhaps you will continue to suffer with these problems, or maybe God will heal you, but one thing is certain: He will restore your life and cause you to be useful to Him. Don't throw in the towel—He's waiting to help.

The Price He Paid

Let's look again at 1 Corinthians 6:19-20: "Do you not know that your body is a temple of the Holy Spirit who is in you, whom you have from God, and that you are not your own? For you have been bought with a price: therefore glorify God in your body."

How is it that God has claimed the right to ownership of your body? And what was the cost of this purchase?

We who are Christians have been ransomed or purchased by the sacred blood of Jesus Christ, the Son of God. It benefits us, when thinking about the cost to God for us, to take ourselves back to Calvary, back to the cross, where our precious, loving Lord suffered and died. Because Jesus paid such a price, not only for our bodies but also for our souls, we should seek to exalt Him in everything. We should not allow any sin to defile the sanctuary where He has chosen, by His Spirit, to reside. Let us remember "the sighs, and tears, and groans that bought us . . . the agonies of the cross, and the bitter pains of the death of God's own Son."[3] If we do so, we know that we must live for God, and for Him alone.

When we are tempted to sin, let us think of the cross. When Satan spreads out his allurements, let us recall the remembrance of the sufferings of Calvary, and remember that all these sorrows were endured so that we might be pure. *O how would sin appear were we beneath the cross, and did we feel*

*the warm blood from the Saviour's open veins
trickle upon us? Who would dare indulge in sin
there? Who could do otherwise than devote himself,
body, and soul, and spirit, unto God?*[4]

Stop for a moment now and reflect upon these words. When you are considering whether you should starve the body that God has given to you, think about Jesus on the cross. When you are thinking about stuffing down those extra slices of pizza, in defiance of His desire for you to be temperate in all things, think about Jesus on the cross. When you are considering another binge and the inevitable purge that will follow, think about Jesus, your Savior, on the cross. Let that terribly beautiful vision of His love control you.

Reflect on the price that your Lord paid to acquire you. It was His very life. ". . . nothing else could or would have done this. There was no PRICE which the sinner could pay, no atonement which HE could make."[5] But now, you are His. "See how great a love the Father has bestowed upon us."[6] "God demonstrates His own love toward us, in that while we were yet sinners, Christ died for us."[7] His love and mercy are so great! We can rest in His arms and know that our body, such as it is, can be used by Him in His exquisitely awesome plan.

LOVE
*to*EAT

H*a*TE
*to*EAT

5

WHY WE DO
WHAT WE DO

"Whom have I in heaven but Thee?
And besides Thee, I desire nothing on earth."

—PSALM 73:25

*E*very morning I get up with a new resolve that today I'm going to do better with my eating," Janet said. "I pray that God will help me and sometimes I make it till dinner, but then I find myself eating whatever I want again. I know what I should and shouldn't eat—what dieter doesn't?—but I find myself wanting to eat some certain thing, and before I know it, it's done. I figure, *Why bother? I've blown it anyway* and I just go for it. The more that I do this, the more discouraged I become and I just give up for a few days or even weeks, and then I start all over again. Why do I eat this way? I don't want to, but I can't seem to break out of this cycle. It seems that I really do love to eat . . . and yet, I hate it!"

A Crucial Question

Have you ever wondered why you do the things that you do? Have you ever wondered why, for instance, it is hard for you to eat in a disciplined manner when other people seem to spend very little time thinking about food at all?

Theories of Motivation

How you answer the question of motivation—why you do what you do—will have some very significant consequences in your life. Since there are many theories of motivation that are generally accepted in our culture, let's take time to look at a few. I'm sure you'll recognize them right away. After we examine what our society is saying about motivation, we'll take a look at what the Bible has to say.

My Mama Made Me Do It

Many people believe that we are *destined* to act in certain ways because of the experiences we encountered in childhood. What that means is that everything we do today somehow has subconscious roots in something that happened to us in our childhood. This is the most common explanation of motivation in our time—I'm sure you've heard newscasters make statements such as, "So-and-so claims that he is not responsible for the murder of his wife because he was raised in a dysfunctional home." Although many in our society have tired of this type of explanation for a person's behavior, it still has a great influence on our thinking.

My Computer Has a Virus

Others believe that man is simply a machine and that the input received will always result in certain corresponding ways of behaving. If I change the input, I am guaranteed a change in the output. The people who believe in this type of motivation or "behaviorism" say that if a parent raises a child in a certain manner, it is practically guaranteed that he will turn out in the expected way. This is the carrot-and-stick theory—the donkey will always pull the wagon if the carrot (reward) is big enough (positive reinforcement) or if the stick (punishment) is substantial enough (negative reinforcement).

Help Me, Doctor, I Think I'm Sick

Many times habitual behaviors such as bulimia and anorexia are referred to as "diseases." Without going into a long discussion on the "medical model" way of looking at things, it is important to understand that bulimia, anorexia, and obesity do have certain physiological *results*. The question that we are considering here, however, is one of motivation. Do women who practice these behaviors have an illness that *causes* them to eat in these harmful ways? Should they look for a pill or injection to cure them, or do they simply need to learn to make different choices? Those who believe eating disorders are diseases say that we do the things we do because of our genes, food allergies, or certain chemicals in the brain (see note #1 for chapter 11 on page 263).

Feel the Force Within You

We live in a spiritual age. Notice I didn't say that we live in a *Christian* age, but a *spiritual* age. All around us today are people who believe that eastern philosophies and mysticism hold the answers to motivation and healthy behavior. Even some Christians believe that they need to discover their "resident inner power" and then clear the obstructions to this power through visualization, positive declarations, and energy direction. They teach that if you are struggling with some unwanted behavior, it is because you're not listening to your inner guidance, and you must change your energy through positive declarations.[2]

The Devil Made Me Do It

Among Christians there is a segment of people who believe that all besetting sins—those behaviors that we seem to struggle with continually—are directly caused by spirits or demons. These Christians say that those who are struggling with difficulties may need to attend a meeting where demons are cast out, where spirits of anorexia, gluttony, or bulimia are being exorcised. But does the devil really hold this kind of power over believers? I don't believe that this is the picture that is painted in the New Testament, where we never see a link made between certain types of sin in a person's life and a corresponding demonic activity and demons that are responsible for causing those same types of sin. In other words, the Bible does not support the idea of a demon of lust, a demon of gluttony, and so on. "Sin is not identified as the cause of demonization; neither is demonization linked to perpetuating sin."[2]

I Don't Love Myself Enough

Another strongly influential explanation for undesirable behavior is low self-esteem. Adherents to this theory teach that the reason you don't act appropriately is lack of self-love. If you could just learn to love and accept yourself as you should, then you wouldn't try to punish yourself or reward yourself inappropriately. Inside of you is the power to love and accept yourself, and this power is strong enough to change you.

It's Not My Fault!

What do you notice about each of these explanations? Although they are all very different in their underlying principles, every single one places the responsibility for undesirable behavior on some *outside* force—your parents, your environment, an illness, your blocked energy flow, the devil, or even inability to love yourself (usually caused by your parents)! "You aren't responsible for your behavior," seems to be the manifesto of our society. But is that what the Bible teaches?

Each of the explanations we just reviewed ignores the truth that one day we will stand before God to give an account of our actions: "So then each one of us shall give account of himself to God" (Romans 14:12). No matter who we are, or what our background is, we will all have to stand before God. While we can all rest in the wonderful reality that we serve a merciful King who loves us with an everlasting love, we cannot disregard His holiness and justice by ignoring our sin and justify ungodly behavior by saying that it's not our fault. No, the same God who has forgiven us through His Son's work on the cross has called us to trust and obey Him . . . by His grace.

Taking Responsibility . . . with God's Grace

God knows our shortcomings and yet He calls us to commitment and holiness. He can do this because He is the One who will supply both the desire and the strength to obey Him. I know it's true that some of us have had to grow up in a more challenging environment than others. I'm not ignoring that fact. *It's just that I believe the Bible teaches that God's grace is stronger than our past.* In fact, I'm sure He delights in taking people who, humanly speaking, have no chance, and making them trophies of His grace. Remember how Paul described those whom God called?

> God has chosen the foolish things of the world to shame the wise, and God has chosen the weak things of the world to shame the things which are strong, and the base things of the world and the despised, God has chosen, the things that are not, that He might nullify the things that are, that no man should boast before God (1 Corinthians 1:27-29).

Does your past cause you to feel foolish, weak, base, or despised? Do you believe that something in your past stops you from living a life that would please God? He loves to glorify Himself through people just like you! This truth is so precious, especially to those who have had difficult child-hoods. Why not read over 1 Corinthians 1:27-29 again? When Paul said that "God has chosen . . . the base things," he was talking about "a person without kin," or someone of unknown descent. You might think, *I don't have a family—I never knew my father. I come from a family of nobodies.* You're just the kind of person God wants to use! I know that some of us use the reasoning that we eat because nobody loved us when we were children. You don't have to think of yourself in that way any longer. God delights in calling you His child, in making you His daughter, *because* you didn't have "all the advantages" that others might have.

When Paul says that God uses "the despised" to glorify Himself, he means those who, in the world's eyes, are contemptible, least esteemed, worthless. The Lord does this so that no one can boast about anything but Him! He does this so that no one can say, "I'm useful to God today because my childhood was almost perfect." No, we have to say, "I'm striving to be useful to God because *He's* so perfect and He's redeeming my past." And that's just what He wants from us—our praise.

If you are in Christ, why not begin today to ask God to show you how He redeems your past and uses it for His glory? The thought that God arranged your history to happen exactly the way it has so that He could turn your mourning into dancing by His grace should fill you with hope and joy.

A Biblical Answer

In chapter 2, I said I believed that the Bible is the *only* standard that can help us know who God is and what He wants from us. Not only does the Bible speak meaningfully about the nature and person of God, but it also teaches profoundly about our own nature. It tells me who I am, why I do the things I do, what I need to do to change.

Although most Christians are quick to agree that the Bible is their source of truth, some have never really grasped the implications of this belief. We see evidence of this in the "explanations" we just looked at for why people have eating problems. Not only do these explanations lack any element of personal responsibility, but they also see, more or less, every individual as being completely unique from all other people.

Your initial response may be, "Well, isn't it true that we're all unique? We're all so different!" Yes . . . we are different. However, though we are unique when it comes to our differing histories, talents, and dispositions, we all share one thing in common: *We all share the same basic human nature.* In many ways we are all very different, but at heart, in the most important ways, we are all exactly the same. We find this clearly affirmed in the Bible.

What the Bible Teaches About Us

The Bible teaches that all people were created in the image of God (Genesis 1:27), that this image in us has been completely marred by sin and the fall (Romans 5:19), and that this image is being restored in the life of believers (Ephesians 4:24). At heart we are all basically the same, while our histories do affect our present motivation and behavior. Yes, we are all substantially influenced by our past and our present. We do respond to our environment. But, even in the face of all these factors, we really are not that unique.

What the Bible Can Do for Us

It is because of this common ground that the Bible can minister dynamically to all people, in all cultures, at all times. It is because of this that I can write with confidence to you no matter where you are or what eating problem you have. God's Word is just as relevant to the inner-city grandmother as it is to the single college student in the Midwest, and to me in my Southern California home. The Bible still speaks truth into every heart just as powerfully as it did 2,000 years ago in the cities in the Holy Land.

You can rejoice in the truth that whoever you are, wherever you are, the Word of God is just as applicable and powerful for you as it is for me. I would despair if I thought that, because of my history or environment, the Word of God would be ineffectual. Where could I go for lasting, God-honoring help if my background put me outside of the reach of the power of the Word? How would I know where the truth *for me* was? I'm thrilled that I can answer with Peter, "Lord, to whom shall we go? You have words of eternal life" (John 6:68). You can thank God that He can be just as powerful in your life as He is in mine. You needn't look outside the Bible for methods to help you understand or change your behavior. The psalmist knew this truth when he wrote, "From Thy precepts I get understanding . . ." (Psalm 119:104). You can have understanding, too. Now, just what does the Bible say about our behaviors, our motives?

Why We Do What We Do

In the New Testament the apostle James gives us one clue as to why we do what we do. He writes, "Each one is tempted when he is carried away and enticed by his own lust" (James 1:14). The first thing we notice in that verse is that we are tempted to sin because each of us have certain "lusts" that reside in our heart. These lusts act as strong stimulants, causing us to view certain temptations as alluring, inviting.

At this point, please don't misunderstand what the word "lust" meant in the New Testament. In our society, "lust" usually has a sexual connotation. That's not the case in James 1:14, however. This word "lust" as used by James actually means *any* strong longing or desire. In its common usage, it can mean either a too-strong desire for something good—for instance, a desire for food (which is God-given) that gets out of control and becomes a lust to overeat; or it can mean a desire that in itself is always wicked, such as lusting after another woman's husband. These "lusts" or strong desires are very powerful motivators of our behavior. The question that needs to be considered when you find yourself overeating, for example, is, "What desire is motivating this behavior?" or, "Just what desire is it that I'm trying to satisfy by eating my third bowl of ice cream?"

When you begin to ask yourself questions such as these, you might find yourself frustrated and confused. How can we know what desires are lurking in our own heart? How do we learn what our desires are, what temptations are most dangerous for us?

The Condition of Our Heart

Here on the heels of telling you that you need to closely examine your own heart and its desires, I have to tell you that no one can ever *fully* know his or her own heart. This inability to rightly discern our own motives, our own heart, is due to our basic nature. The nature of our heart is described in Jeremiah 17:9, which says that the heart is deceitful and wicked and that only God truly knows it. This thought is repeated in other Scripture passages, including 2 Chronicles 6:30: ". . . for Thou alone dost know the hearts of the sons of men."[3] Only God is wise and discerning enough to look past all of our deception and see us as we are. This is because of our natural self-love. We tend to overlook the wickedness resident in our heart—we are fooled into thinking that we really aren't that bad after all . . . we certainly aren't as bad as so-and-so down the street. This is exactly what the writer of Hebrews means when he states that our hearts can be "hardened by the deceitfulness of sin" (Hebrews 3:13).

We all know people who have been seriously deceived by sin yet who tell us that what they are doing is perfectly fine. How does that happen? Sin speaks to us in our hearts, telling us that the wrong we are planning is right. We become hardened to true wisdom. When we look into our own heart, all we can see is our own excuses and rationalizations. We are self-deceived, and it's this self-deception that makes it difficult to know ourselves. For instance, how many times have I found myself being critical and judgmental of some other Christian only to find myself doing exactly the same thing? How many times have I thought, *I'm better than so-and-so*, only to find myself entrapped in the same behavior? Thank God for His mercy and patience! Although we can never fully know our own hearts, our desires, our weaknesses, our areas of temptations, we must strive to grow in this area.[4]

It is because of this propensity to gloss over our own sinfulness that we come to our second principle: The *only* way for us to understand the desires that play into our temptations is to spend time in the Word. Consider again this verse from Hebrews 4:12:

> The word of God is living and active and
> sharper than any two-edged sword, and piercing as
> far as the division of soul and spirit, of both joints
> and marrow, and able to judge the thoughts and
> intentions of the heart.

It is only as we interact with the Word of God that we find ourselves growing in our ability to judge our own thoughts and intentions. Only the Bible can help us to gain the wisdom that we so desperately need. It is only as we find ourselves in the pages of Scripture that we know what our personal desires and temptations are. This is one of the primary functions of the Bible—Paul himself said that he would not know that he coveted nor that coveting was sinful (Romans 7:7) unless he had discovered this truth in the law. God's Word brings light to us and gives us understanding even of the dark corners of our heart.[5]

The third principle in understanding our own heart is prayer. Jesus counseled His followers to "keep watching and praying, that you may not enter into temptation; the spirit is willing, but the flesh is weak" (Matthew 26:41). "Watching"involves being aware or spiritually alert to those areas of temptation that are most dangerous for you personally. You must learn to pray that God would teach you what the areas of your strongest desires are. For instance, if you have a strong desire to have people tell you that you look good, you may be tempted to force yourself to vomit when you have eaten more than you should. We'll talk more about pinpointing specific desires in a moment.

In His greatest hour of trial, Jesus lovingly counseled His disciples to pray that they might not enter into temptation. Along with praying that God would enable you to understand what your particular areas of temptation are, you'll want to pray that you would be kept alert when they are present so you don't succumb to them. Only the Holy Spirit can enable you to resist temptation, and you'll find your ability to resist strengthened through prayer. I have found that very few people actually pray that they be kept from particular temptations before they come upon them. Yes, we might pray *when* we are being tempted, but how often do we pray beforehand? How many heartaches might be avoided if we would learn to pray *before* we are tempted!

Returning to our passage from James 1, we see that temptation to sin does not originate with God. "Let no one say when he is tempted, 'I am being tempted by God'; for God cannot be tempted by evil, and He Himself does not tempt anyone" (James 1:13). Temptations come to us from outside ourselves, from the world (including media pressures, peer pressures, materialism, secularism), and from the devil. Inwardly temptations spring out of our own flesh (our own personal desires—emotional, physical, intellectual). It is when the allurements of the world or Satan find a connection with the desires of our own hearts that we are enticed to sin. Ungodly influences would not be effective if our hearts were pure from sinful desires. That is why Satan was unsuccessful in his temptation of Christ. Satan could find nothing, no ungodly desire to latch on to (John 14:30).

The reason those television commercials for "sinfully rich" desserts or sizzling hot burgers can cause us to stumble is because of certain desires within our own hearts. We could watch a movie about robbing banks and never be tempted one bit to do the same because there are no corresponding desires in our hearts. But are there other allurements that work in combination with the discontent or greed in our hearts that might motivate use to sin? Of course. That's why it's so important for use to know what our personal desires are, and then to avoid situations where we might be strongly tempted to give in to them.

Recognizing Ungodly Desires

Love of Independence

Sometimes our eating habits reflect a desire in our hearts to be free from any restraint. It is the desire to have what we want when we want it. Advertisers for fast-food restaurants exploit this desire when they tell you that you have the right to "have it your way." You shouldn't have to wait; you shouldn't have to compromise; you deserve to have exactly what you want! Why do advertisers appeal in this way to us? Because we respond.

We often demonstrate this heart of self-sufficient independence with statements like, "No one is going to tell me what I can and cannot eat," or "You can't make me eat that food," or "Everything in my life is so out of control—this is the only area that I get to do what I want!" Scripture reminds us, however, that only the Lord has this right and the power to control. We humans have been trying to "have it our way" since the Garden of Eden. This desire to be god or be in control is nothing new; it's the same desire that arose in Eve when she succumbed to the serpent's enticement.

Love of Pleasure

Recently I reread C.S. Lewis' *Space Trilogy* series. In the second book, *Perelandra*, I discovered another key to the problem of sinful eating. The hero, Ransom, finds himself on one of the floating islands on the planet of Perelandra. He is hungry and happens to walk through a grove of trees that have fruit hanging from them. This is how Lewis describes Ransom's experience:

> He picked one of them and turned it over and over. The rind was smooth and firm and seemed impossible to tear open. Then by accident one of his fingers punctured it and went through into coldness. After a moment's hesitation he put the little aperture to his lips. He had meant to extract the smallest, experimental sip, but the first taste put his caution to all flight. It was, of course, a taste, just as his thirst and hunger had been thirst and hunger. But then it was so different from every other taste that it seemed mere pedantry to call it a taste at all. It was like the discovery of a totally new genus of pleasures, something unheard of among men. . . . As he let the empty gourd fall from his hand and was about to pluck a second one, it came into his head that he was now neither hungry nor thirsty. And yet to repeat a pleasure so intense and almost so spiritual seemed an obvious thing to do. His reason . . . was all in favor of tasting this miracle again; the childlike innocence of fruit, the labors he had undergone, the uncertainty of the future, all seemed to commend the action. Yet something seemed opposed to this "reason." . . . he stood pondering over this and wondering how often in his life on

earth he had reiterated pleasures not through desire, but in the teeth of desire."[6]

Lewis captures the heart of sinful pleasure-seeking— the desire to experience some form of pleasure just for the sake of trying to greedily recreate the episode, rather than for its given purpose. Is it wrong to eat food and enjoy it? No, certainly not. If that were the case, the Lord would not have blessed us with the capacity to taste. It is wrong to eat only when the purpose of that eating is simply to experience the pleasure of the crunch or the sweetness or the temperature *in spite of* God's good provision. It is the heart that says, "I know this is more than I need, and that I'm harming myself by having it, but I love the pleasure of this experience more than I love the pleasure of doing what pleases the Lord, so I'm just going to go ahead and satiate myself."

Cultivating Godly Desires

The Biblical Instructions

The place to start in changing your lifestyle is to look at your desires and seek to change them. What are the kinds of desires that God wants you to have? Let's look at a few verses from the Old Testament that speak about where our desires are to be centered (emphasis added):

- "Whom have I in heaven but Thee? And *besides Thee, I desire nothing on earth*" (Psalm 73:25).

- "*I stretch out my hands to Thee; my soul longs for Thee*, as a parched land" (Psalm 143:6).

- "At night my *soul longs for Thee,* indeed, my spirit within me seeks Thee diligently" (Isaiah 26:9).

- "*My soul thirsts for God, for the living God;* when shall I come and appear before God?" (Psalm 42:2).

- "O God, Thou art my God; I shall seek Thee earnestly; m*y soul thirsts for Thee, my flesh yearns for Thee,* in a dry and weary land where there is no water" (Psalm 63:1).

Isn't it interesting that these writers who were inspired by the Holy Spirit used words such as "thirsts," "longs," and "desire" to talk about their relationship with God? Does that describe your pursuit of Him? I know that many times I have longed for a drink of water or yearned to eat a certain kind of food—I have desired to go to a certain restaurant and insisted on "having it my way." But do I long, yearn, and thirst in the same way for God? You know, if we would seek our satisfaction wholly in Him, we would find true pleasure and joy. Pleasures beyond measure . . . endless rivers of joy. That's what the Bible teaches in Psalm 16:11: "Thou wilt make known to me the path of life; *in Thy presence is fulness of joy; in Thy right hand there are pleasures forever*" (emphasis added).

This is also what Jesus meant when He taught, "Blessed are those who *hunger* and *thirst* for righteousness, for they shall be satisfied" (Matthew 5:6, emphasis added). The word "blessed" has lost a lot of its meaning in our modern language. In the New Testament it is a rich word that has the idea of the highest good, to be supremely blest—happy, fortunate, well off. Do you understand what Jesus is saying to you? If you are hungry and thirsty for anything but Him, if you desire pleasures or power instead of Him, you will never be satisfied. But if you desire Him, you will be supremely happy because you will find satisfaction! This satisfaction that Jesus speaks of is no miserly pittance. It is an abundant satisfaction. It literally means "to gorge"! Here's a paraphrase of Matthew 5:6: "You will be supremely happy, blest, and fortunate if you desire Jesus and His righteousness, for if that is your desire, you will be utterly gorged!" Isn't that exciting?

C.S. Lewis knew this. He believed that we were too easily satisfied with the "lesser joys" of life instead of pressing on to pure, full joy in Christ. He wrote, "We are half-hearted creatures, fooling about with drink and sex and ambition [and food] when infinite joy is offered us, like an ignorant child who wants to go on making mud pies in a slum because he cannot imagine what is meant by the offer of a holiday at the sea. We are far too easily pleased."[7]

Solomon, the wisest man who ever lived, knew this principle. Thousands of years ago he wrote, "All a man's labor is for his mouth and yet the appetite is not satisfied" (Ecclesiastes 6:7). Think of that! How much of our life has been focused on our appetite—an appetite that ultimately does not remain satisfied? Only if our appetite is for Him will we be satisfied.

The Biblical Illustration

The nature of desires is that they are never filled, there is never enough. That's the principle that was at work in the hearts of the Israelites in the desert. Psalm 78 is a retelling of their history. The lust of God's chosen people was not satisfied with Him (His presence was tangibly with them in the cloud and the fire), nor with His provision (manna). They longed for food from Egypt. "Just a couple of garlics . . . just some pots of meat . . . just some savory flavors."[8] The psalmist describes it this way: "In their heart they put God to the test by asking food according to their desire" (Psalm 78:18). They wanted meat to eat. So, God sent them meat (quail to be exact), and judged them for their desires. He didn't send His wrath upon the Israelites because it was wrong to eat food, but because they were unbelieving and seeking their joy in something other than Him. Their appetite was "insatiable; they were well filled and yet they were not satisfied. Such is the nature of lust; it is content with nothing,"[9] and the more it is fed, the hungrier it grows. "Those that indulge their lust will never be estranged from it."[10] Here they were, being sustained by the presence of the living God in a wilderness, but still they complained and cried about the fare God provided. The ending of this story is very shocking: The passage tells us that while the food was still in their mouths, while they were rolling it around under their tongue, "the wrath of God came upon them, and slew the fattest of them" (Psalm 78:31 KJV).[11]

I remember the first time that I read those verses and understood what God was saying. How can it be that a loving, merciful God would so judge His chosen nation?

God *is* loving—in fact, He is so loving the Bible says that "He is love."[12] Why would this loving God demand that we seek our satisfaction in Him alone? Why would He thwart all of our attempts to be happy without Him? It is simply *because* He is loving that He does this. If He knows that He is the only source of true pleasure and satisfaction, then it would be unloving of Him to allow us to go on our merry ways, trying to satisfy ourselves without Him, knowing all the while that our lives will end in futility and despair. The lessons that are recorded in Psalm 78 are written by a hand of love. Are we willing to learn the lesson He is teaching?

A Wonderful Assurance

Take time to rejoice in the assurance that God offers. All of your godly desires—in fact, *everything* that you need—will be abundantly satisfied in Him. Will you seek Him? If you do, you will find Him and His presence so satisfying that you will wonder why you ever doubted Him. Will you say with the psalmist, "There is nothing on earth that I desire besides You"? If so, you will find "fullness of joy . . . [and] pleasures forever" (Psalm 16:11). Don't misunderstand and think that the joys of this earth are worth sacrificing for. This verse promises fullness or completeness of joy—the word "joy" in Psalm 16:11 means a great mirth, making a feast before God!

Do you want to have a great party with gleeful dancing, rejoicing, and feasting, all without sin or guilt? You can have that now, in a shadowy measure, as you commune with Him—and in an overwhelming, breathtaking measure in heaven as you ceaselessly exult in the exceeding sweetness of His glory at the greatest party of all time, the Marriage Supper of the Lamb!

Won't you put aside your mud pies . . . and feast on Him alone?

6

GOD'S LIFE-CHANGING POWER

"You were taught regarding your previous habit patterns to put off the old person that you were, who is corrupted by deceitful desires, being rejuvenated in the attitude of your mind, and to put on the new person that you are, who is created in God's likeness with righteousness and holiness that come from the truth...."

—EPHESIANS 4:22-24
THE CHRISTIAN COUNSELOR'S COMMENTARY[1]

We have spent a lot of time examining the foundation for proper eating and some of the reasons why we struggle in this area. I know this has been a lot for you to get through, but I am longing for you to really understand what I believe are underlying truths about our eating habits. Congratulations! You've finally made it.

I also know that you wouldn't have picked up this book unless you are a person who both loves and hates to eat. I know that you are looking for answers to this dilemma and it is here, in this chapter, that I hope to introduce them to you.

The pages of the Bible are filled with the histories of people whose lives have been changed. If you're like me, you've looked at these examples and wondered why change hasn't been more apparent in your life. I under-stand this. It's discouraging to struggle year after year with the same problem and never see any real change. What is the solution to this? Does the Bible mark out a path for us to follow?

Bringing About Real Change

A Different Sort of Change

What I'm about to tell you will, at first, seem very simplistic. Please strive to remember everything that I've said so far about the power and sufficiency of God's Word because I believe that what I'm going to tell you is His plan, not mine.

Aside from seeming simplistic, this method may also seem too difficult and time-consuming. If you're like me, you want instant change. I have wished thousands (millions?) of times that God would just touch my life in such a way that I wouldn't have to struggle with sin any longer. *Can't you just make me better instantly?* I wonder. It is this desire to be freed from sin that makes me long for heaven. While I'm still here though, I know that the Lord has reasons for allowing me to continue in this struggle, not the least of which is my personal growth in humility and dependence upon Him. I've come to realize that my impa-tience is partly due to my own pride and laziness. But still, practicing godly principles is not easy, and you may grow weary in it. We'll talk more about perseverance later; for now, let me encourage you by saying that while there may be times when you feel like giving up, God will never give up on you. Philippians 1:6 promises that "he who began a good work in you will carry it on to completion" (NIV).

The Biblical Method of Change

As in all of God's creation, there is an order, a process, and gradual growth in His method for your change—or what the Bible calls your *sanctification*. I believe that God's method for your sanctification (change) is summed up in these four basic steps:

> *Relying upon the Holy Spirit, you must:*
>
> 1. *Become convinced that your present method of eating is sinful and cease from it;*
>
> 2. *Become convinced that God's methods for disciplined eating are right and begin practicing them;*
>
> 3. *Seek diligently to change your mind and become conformed to God's thinking, especially in the area of your eating habits; and*
>
> 4. *Continue to practice these new thoughts and behaviors, even when the struggle gets hard.*

Now you can see why I warned that this can seem both simplistic and too difficult! You may be saying, "So you're telling me that I just need to stop eating wrongly, start eating righteously, and keep trying until I've got it? You've got to be kidding!" Before you come to such a conclusion, let me explain exactly what is involved . . . and exactly how you can accomplish this. I know you'll need concrete steps and practical examples to help you get a clear idea of how God brings true change into our lives. I'll plainly lay this plan out for you. But for now, before you give up in despair, thinking that these steps are just too difficult, remember that you can be confident in God's help. I too have struggled with my own sinful eating habits in the light of God's Word and I've found specific answers. I'm no different than you. God will enable you to obey Him—remember it's *His* desire to change you!

The Foundation of Change

What we tend to overlook in this whole process of change is the foundation: relying upon the Holy Spirit.

Hang in there for a few more pages while I encourage you about the power and comfort that God's Spirit can bring to you.

The Spirit's Comfort and Control

Both you and I know that neither one of us is able to effect any real change in our own lives. Yes, people do go on diets and lose weight, quit smoking, and take up tennis. I know that even unregenerate people have successfully achieved change for the good in their lives, but these changes are not the change of heart that pleases God. *Remember, our goal is not to look good outwardly; our goal is to be conformed to the image of Christ for God's glory.* You can't do that through a program of self-rejuvenation. A counselor or special diet drink can't accomplish your sanctification. A new diet book can't either. No, this change is achieved only through the power of the Holy Spirit. Remember, it's one of the results (fruit) of the Spirit's work,[2] *self-discipline,* that we're after here.

Appreciating the Spirit's Ministry in Your Life

The Holy Spirit is the most effective agent for change in all of creation. He is eternal and omnipresent. When He moved over the waters at God's command, the earth and all that we see was formed. When He overshadowed Mary, she conceived our Savior. He worked mightily through Christ's life, and even accomplished His resurrection. In fact, your own personal regeneration was accomplished by the work of the Holy Spirit. The Spirit took you when you were dead in your sins and, by His power, made you alive! And as your Counselor, He comforts you, pours His love through you, and fills your heart with joy. This is the Spirit that has been sent to you by your loving Father. This is the Spirit that indwells you. This is the Spirit that can accomplish every God-pleasing change that you are longing for.

On page 83, I listed four steps for God's method of bringing change into your life. Let's begin taking a closer look at each step, and see how the Holy Spirit is involved in each one.

Step One: Become convinced that
your present method of eating is
sinful and cease from it.

The Holy Spirit is the one who convicts or convinces you of sin: "And He, when He comes, will convict the world concerning sin, and righteousness, and judgment" (John 16:8). Without a work of God's grace by His Spirit in our lives, we'll never appraise anything that we do as truly sinful. We might not like it, and we might think that it is inconvenient, but . . . sinful? That's something different. Thank God that He has sent His Spirit to indwell us so that we can learn to differentiate between good and evil: "Solid food [strong truth] is for the mature, who because of practice have their senses trained to discern good and evil" (Hebrews 5:14). The Holy Spirit will train you to know the difference between righteous and unrighteous eating as you grow in your practice of godliness. No, you won't understand everything right away. But you can be confident that as the Spirit trains you in truth, you will grow in your ability to discern good and evil.

The Holy Spirit will also enable you to stop carrying out the desire of the flesh that you exhibit with your eating: "If *by the Spirit* you are *putting to death the deeds of the body*, you will live" (Romans 8:13, emphasis added). It is the Spirit that empowers you to put to death both your sinful desires and sinful deeds. You know that you can't do it on your own. Only the mighty power of the Spirit can slay the dragon of our sin. Think again about how great His power is! Think back on other victories He has gotten for you in your life. His power is the same today as it was then.

Step Two: Become convinced that God's methods for disciplined eating are right and begin practicing them.

The Holy Spirit is the only one who can teach you the truth: "When He, the Spirit of truth, comes, He will guide you into all the truth" (John 16:13). Only He can teach you how to eat in a way that is pleasing to Him. In an upcoming chapter of this book I will give you a grid for discerning godly eating habits, but as far as learning exactly what is pleasing to the Lord, both in your outward behavior and also in your heart, if there is going to be any God-pleasing change, it has to come from Him. Don't despair though— it's His *delight* to teach you how to love God with your whole heart, soul, mind, and strength.

It is only the Holy Spirit who, once He has taught you the truth, can bring about real change: ". . . God has chosen you from the beginning for salvation through sanctification *by the Spirit* and faith in the truth" (2 Thessalonians 2:13, emphasis added); it is He that accomplishes the sanctifying work (change) in you. You've been "chosen according to the foreknowledge of God the Father, *by the sanctifying work of the Spirit*, that you may obey Jesus Christ . . ." (1 Peter 1:1-2, emphasis added). Did you notice that in both of those verses, it's the Holy Spirit who works with the Father to sanctify you? You see, it's not God's plan that you remain the same after your conversion. He hasn't merely chosen you for salvation; He's also chosen you for sanctification. He wants to change you so that your life will be more and more of a praise to Him. And the agent He uses to accomplish this gradual transformation is the Spirit.

Accomplishing your change is part of the Holy Spirit's job description. Remember, if He can raise you from spiritual deadness, He can certainly accomplish this work of grace.

Step Three: Seek diligently to change your mind and become conformed to God's thinking, especially in the area of your eating habits.

It is only as we are taught by the Spirit to put off our old deeds and to put on new ones that our thinking really changes. This change in the way that you think happens throughout this entire process, from beginning to end. Here's how Paul described this change:

> Lay aside the old self [your old, sinful way of eating], which is being corrupted in accordance with the lusts of deceit [springing out of your sinful desires], and . . . be *renewed in the spirit of your mind* [the way that you think about food and eating needs to change], and put on the new self [new, godly ways of eating], which in the likeness of God [being changed into His image] has been created in righteousness and holiness of the truth [that the Holy Spirit is creating in you] (Ephesians 4:22-24, emphasis added).

As you can see, the Holy Spirit is involved in every aspect of this process. It is He who convinces, informs, changes, and enlightens you. Changing the way that you think about Him, about yourself, and about eating is key to this process. Only the Holy Spirit knows God's thoughts and can reveal them to you:

> Who among men knows the thoughts of a man except the spirit of the man, which is in him? Even so the thoughts of God no one knows except the Spirit of God. Now we have received, not the spirit

of the world, but the Spirit who is from God, that we might know the things freely given to us by God. . . . For who has known the mind of the Lord, that he should instruct Him? But we have the mind of Christ (1 Corinthians 2:11-12,16).

No one but the Holy Spirit, using His Word, can teach you about the way that God thinks. Godly authors and Bible teachers can endeavor to explain God's truth to you, but only the Spirit can bring revelation and conviction. Only the Spirit can write His law on the tablets of your heart and make you long to know and obey it.

How does He accomplish this task? The Spirit teaches you primarily through the Word He authored:

- "The commandment is a lamp, and the teaching is light . . ." (Proverbs 6:23).

- "The law of the LORD is perfect, restoring the soul; the testimony of the LORD is sure, making wise the simple" (Psalm 19:7).

- "The unfolding of Thy words gives light; it gives understanding to the simple" (Psalm 119:130).

You will have light, restoration, wisdom, and understanding as you meditate on His Word under the anointing of His presence. Bible reading is important, but reading page after page of the Bible won't change your heart. That's why people in universities can study the Bible as a historical document or work of literature and never be influenced by it at all. You must not only read, but also pray for wisdom as you read each passage, and ask God to send His Spirit to enlighten your understanding so that you can know what God meant in a particular passage.

My practice is to read through the Bible every year. But my daily reading does absolutely nothing for me if I don't take time to pray and ask God to open His Word to me.

Then I must think about (meditate on) what I'm reading and try to grasp how it applies to my life. The Holy Spirit accomplishes all that for me.

Step Four: Continue to practice these new thoughts and behaviors, even when the struggle gets hard.

This is where most of us fail. We start out enthusiastically, filled with the hope that things are finally going to be different. But after a few days we find ourselves back in the same rut again, and we give up or run off to find another answer. I can't tell you how many times I've done this. I would read a new diet book, think that it sounded reasonable, practice it for a few days (or weeks), tire of it, and then go in search of something else. I'm proposing something entirely different here. I'm proposing that what we need is a Spirit-wrought godliness, not just another diet. The "practice" of godliness that the Spirit is working in us is the *only* solution that's going to have true and lasting results.

The Spirit's Ministry to You

Are you to the point in your struggles where you feel like giving up hope? Do you feel as if you're just never going to succeed? I can tell you from personal experience—and from the testimonies of many women who have struggled as you and I have—that the only source of hope is the work of the Holy Spirit. You *can* persevere . . . you *can* have hope . . . when you rest solely on the Spirit's help. Let's see why that is so.

Sealing You Until the Day of Redemption

There are several reasons you can have hope. First, remember that it is the Holy Spirit who has sealed you until the day that you are freed from all sins. It is by the Holy

Spirit that "you were sealed for the day of redemption" (Ephesians 4:30).

This concept of God sealing us by His Spirit is so beautiful, let me take a moment to explain it to you. In ancient times, whenever a sack of grain or trunk of goods was sent somewhere, the sender placed a wax seal on the package— a seal that was imprinted with the insignia on the sender's personal ring. This seal had several purposes: it indicated that the contents of the package was authentic, the real thing; it stopped thieves from removing anything from the package until it arrived safely at its destination; it distinguished the package from others.

You, dear friend, are a package sealed by the Holy Spirit. You are on your way to a specific destination. If the Holy Spirit is in you, God has indicated that you are the real thing, you're not a make-believer or a fake-believer—you really are His child! The Holy Spirit acts as a guard to keep anyone away who might try to steal you out of your Father's hand. The Spirit also sets you apart from others who say that they are on their way to heaven but really aren't.

Yes, the Holy Spirit has sealed you to ensure that you are safely delivered to your destination. He is a foretaste of all the joys and glories of redemption, and you have your Father's promise that He will be with you until the day that you enter His presence.

The Holy Spirit's sealing power over you should encourage you. Yes, it will be hard to struggle with your sin—but you are not alone! You don't have to give up in frustration when you fail, thinking that you need to find some other method, some new diet, some "magic bullet." God's Word is powerful, and although the struggle against sin will not end until you get to heaven, you can rest in the knowledge that God's power is strong enough to strengthen you, change you, and carry on that process to its ultimate consummation, when you arrive home in heaven.

Filling You with Hope

While you are involved in this struggle, you can be cheered by the truth that the Holy Spirit will buoy your sinking heart with hope:

> We also exult in our tribulations, knowing that tribulation brings about perseverance; and perseverance, proven character; and proven character, hope; and hope does not disappoint, because the love of God has been poured out within our hearts through the Holy Spirit who was given to us (Romans 5:3-5).

Yes, even in the midst of the tribulation of learning to eat in a godly way, you can have hope because the Holy Spirit continually in-fills you with the love of God. God's love can encourage, strengthen, enable, and comfort you as you face this struggle for your sanctification. As you rely upon Him, you'll experience this pouring out of God's love into your heart. You needn't be afraid that you won't make it—think about what His love has done for you! After all, "He who did not spare His own Son, but delivered Him up for us all, how will He not also with Him freely give us all things?" (Romans 8:32). If God has already given His all to us by giving His Son, is there anything that He cannot give us? God has already given you an unspeakable gift—the Lord Jesus Christ. Why would He stop you from persevering in your trial? "For the LORD God is a sun and shield; the LORD gives grace and glory; *no good thing does He withhold from those who walk uprightly*" (Psalm 84:11, emphasis added). I believe that eating in a way that glorifies God is a good thing—and because of this, I am confident that He won't withhold from you the knowledge and strength to accomplish this. He wants you to be free more than you do. Rejoice and relax in His wondrous love!

Your Father not only wants you to have hope that you can change, He also wants you to abound in hope—and it's the Holy Spirit's power that will help you do just that: "Now may the God of hope fill you with all joy and peace in believing, that you may *abound in hope* by the power of the Holy Spirit" (Romans 15:13, emphasis added). He doesn't merely want you to hope; He wants you to *super-abound* in hope—to overflow with it, to have more than you can imagine. It's the power of the Spirit that can fill you with hope that true heart-change is possible. You can pray in the same way that Paul did: "God, fill me with all joy and peace. Help me to abound in hope by the power of Your Holy Spirit."

Intercession for Your Needs

You can persevere because you know that the Holy Spirit isn't just some bystander in this struggle. He's not some disinterested war correspondent. No, He's your lifeline to headquarters and He is always helping you: "In the same way the Spirit also helps our weakness; for we do not know how to pray as we should, but the Spirit Himself intercedes for us with groanings too deep for words" (Romans 8:26). There may be times in this battle that you don't even feel as though you know how to pray—you may feel that you are too weak to cry out for help. It's during these times that God has promised that the Spirit will help us by interceding personally on our behalf. Don't give up even if you feel too feeble to pray. Remember that He knows exactly how to pray for you because He knows God's thoughts and is praying for you according to His will.[3] God knows just what you need to get you through the battle, and He's commissioned the Spirit to pray for it.

Provision of Comfort and Strength

God sends His Spirit to comfort and strengthen you, just as He did the Christians in the first century. "The church throughout all Judea and Galilee and Samaria enjoyed peace, being built up; and, going on in the fear of the Lord and in the comfort of the Holy Spirit, it continued to increase" (Acts 9:31). In fact, one of the ways that the Spirit's name is translated in Scripture is *Comforter*. He wants to teach you to comfort yourself not with food, but with *His* comfort. His comfort is so winsome, so whole-some, so encouraging—why go anywhere else?

Fulfilling the Desires of the Spirit

And finally, you can rejoice that He empowers you so that as you "walk by the Spirit . . . you will not carry out the desire of the flesh" (Galatians 5:16). How do we walk by the Spirit? By setting our affections on Him, relying on Him, seeking to please Him, resting and trusting in Him, praying to and worshiping Him, and reading, meditating upon, and obeying His Word. If you are striving to do these things, you will continually grow in your ability to carry out your godly desires and cease to carry out your fleshly ones.

God's Power, Not Ours

Perhaps I have belabored this point a little, but I want you to have confidence that we don't have to accomplish this change by our own willpower. Besides, we both know that we don't have that kind of strength. God desires our change more than we do, and for all the right reasons. It is because He wants our life to glorify Him that He has placed His Spirit within (if you are a Christian), and He *will* accomplish His purpose. In the following chapters, I'll go through each of the steps to change in more detail, so hang in there! For now, think about and meditate upon God's great love for you and the wonderful gift He's given you in the Holy Spirit.

PART THREE

Embracing God's Methods for Change

7

A RIGHT PERSPECTIVE
OF FOOD

*"Do not let sin reign in your mortal body
that you should obey its lusts...."*

—ROMANS 6:12

~~~~~~~

*Y*ou know, my goal from the beginning of this book has been for you to experience the heart-change that comes with knowing and embracing the truth. You may be feeling anxious or impatient, wanting to get to the "diet plan." I can certainly understand this desire. I'm just the same. In the past, when I've read diet books, I've frequently skipped right to the eating plan so that I could get to the store and buy the food on the list and get going. I usually didn't care why I should eat in the ways the authors said; I just wanted to get going on losing some weight.

Even though it might be challenging for you to go through each of these steps, let me gently invite you to patiently work through them and to wait for the Spirit's ministry in your life. I've seen the work that the Holy Spirit can accomplish, and it's so much more desirable than just avoiding sugar for two weeks. So don't get discouraged—it is vitally important that you get God's perspective on your problem. Soon, I'll reveal the grid that you can use in order to develop your discernment for how you ought to eat. But for now, try to remember that our goal is to become conformed to the image of God's Son and thereby to bring Him glory. With that in mind, let's take some time now to go through each one of the four steps we learned one by one in chapter 6. In this chapter, we will look at the first step.

Step One: Become convinced that your present method of eating is sinful and cease from it.

Please know that I'm aware that you are already uncomfortable with your eating habits. You wouldn't have gotten this far in this book if you weren't pretty desperate to find a way out of your problem. But, when I say that you need to become convinced that your eating (or lack of it) is sinful, that is something entirely different from being uncomfortable, embarrassed, or feeling ashamed because others are pressuring you to change your habits. That is not what I'm speaking of either.

Understanding Sin

The concept that I'm going to introduce you to now might be difficult to grasp at first because we live in and have been influenced by a society that has lost an understanding of the definition of sin. In our culture, sin has been redefined either as a crime or a disease.[1] We think of guilt as a negative concept, something to be avoided, rather than God's good gift designed to bring us to repentance. The main reason society has this view is because many people usually don't think about God's perspective on their behavior, nor do they care that their sin just might be an affront to

Him. Even those of us who do think about Him frequently lose sight of God's majestic holiness and His desire for holiness in our lives. In fact, much of what we read and hear in Christian circles today so radically downplays God's holiness and exalts His love (as though the two were not related, the latter only constant because of the former) that Christians hardly have a thought about God's character being *anything but love*.[2]

So then, our first priority is to get a clear picture of God's holiness and His hatred of sin. We can do this by studying verses that talk about His character, such as Exodus 15:11: "Who is like Thee among the gods, O LORD? Who is like Thee, majestic in holiness, awesome in praises, working wonders?" and Habakkuk 1:13: "Thine eyes are too pure to approve evil, and Thou canst not look on wickedness with favor." Then there are passages that speak of God's hatred of sin, such as Romans 1:18: "The wrath of God is revealed from heaven against all ungodliness and unrighteousness of men." We can grow in our understanding of God's holiness and His hatred of sin by studying His Word and asking the Holy Spirit to help us.

Progress toward change (or sanctification), then, requires us to see our overeating, bingeing, or starvation as sin—not just something inconvenient, embarrassing, or troublesome. As we saw earlier, God poured out His wrath on the Israelites because of their gluttony. Yes, gluttony is a sin, just as surely as drunkenness or adultery. We must be convinced of the truth of this statement or we will never hate our sin enough to leave it. If we don't see it as sin, we will try to keep it around (tame, on a leash) and bring it out when no one will be offended.

How much do you want to know the joy of the freedom Christ purchased for you? I want so much for you to know this freedom as I have. Let me gently encourage you to ask—no, *plead* with—the Holy Spirit to convict you of the sinfulness of any gluttonous eating habits you might have. This might be hard for you to do. Perhaps you don't even want to hate your habit yet. If so, then cry to the Lord to give you the desire to hate it.

Do you see that God knows your heart anyway? He knows how you love your sin, and yet He also sees your heart that wants to please Him. He has the power to help you hate your sin because it is sin, not just because it's embarrassing. You see, if you hate your sin only because you feel fat or ashamed, then you'll fall right back into your old ways when you think you don't look bad anymore or when your mom isn't bugging you about not eating. You have to learn to hate any options that let you try to satisfy your desires outside of God love.

Do I Have to Call It Sin?

I know this is hard, but hang in there. Perhaps this is the first time that you have ever been face to face with the reality that your eating habits may be sinful. Please don't be discouraged. I struggled with this as well, as have many women I've talked with.

Determining that some thought, word, or deed you commit is sin is very humiliating. I know this. As I look at my own heart, I don't mind saying that I make mistakes, or have bad habits, or even that I have some problems. I just hate saying that I struggle with some particular sin. Isn't there some other way that I can look at my problems? I could just call them "eating issues," couldn't I? That sounds cleaner, nicer, more palatable. The really sad part of this prideful way of thinking is that it turns me away from the only source of help available. I must always remind myself "that Christ Jesus came into the world to save sinners, among whom I am foremost of all" (1 Timothy 1:15). Instead of devising comfortable euphemisms to describe my problem, I need to fall on the mercy of the One who saves me from sin. Please don't find offense in the use of the words "gluttony" or "sin." I'm not condemning you; I'm seeking to direct you to the One who died for our sins and who is the sole source of every victory over sin—even the sin of gluttony.

What Makes Our Eating Sinful?

Think with me for one moment: Why should we view certain eating practices as sin? Why would God call them sin?

Back to Egypt

Eating habits become sinful when the habitual practice of them places us in bondage again—a bondage to sin from which Christ died to free us. Although it might not be inherently sinful for me to eat a bag of M & M's (certainly there is no direct command in Scripture to abstain from candy) or to force myself to vomit ("Thou shalt not vomit"?), it is sinful for me to habitually give myself over to a behavior that may ultimately enslave me.

Remember Paul's words: "All things are lawful for me, but not all things are profitable. All things are lawful for me, but *I will not be mastered by anything.* Food is for the stomach, and the stomach is for food; but God will do away with both of them" (1 Corinthians 6:12-13, emphasis added).

Paul argues that there are lawful things in the world that must be shunned by Christians because their nature is such that they enslave. For those of us whose desires frequently run to sinful eating habits, we must fervently guard the freedom Christ has purchased. I might be able to eat a brownie every day at least as far as God's moral law is concerned, but I know my heart—if I were to do that, I could very well place myself into slavery again.

It is interesting that Paul uses the example of food and the belly when he talks about this area of Christian liberty. Food is to be eaten, but both food and the body will eventually be done away with and we must not allow either to enslave us or make us unfit for heaven. "The expectation we have of being without bodily appetites in a future life is a very good argument against being under their power in the present life."[3]

Paul encouraged the Roman believers along those same lines:

> Do you not know that when you present your-selves to someone as slaves for obedience, you are slaves of the one whom you obey, either of sin result-ing in death, or of obedience resulting in righteous-ness? . . . For just as you presented your members as slaves to impurity and to lawlessness, resulting in further lawlessness, so now present your members as slaves to righteousness, resulting in sanctification (Romans 6:16,19).

Our hearts are easily enslaved, and when we present our body (our members) to gluttony or other extreme dietary habits, the impact is far more devastating than we might think at the time. We might think, *Oh, just a little of this Turkish Delight won't cause harm.* But you must ask yourself if you are again placing yourself under the rule of someone or something other than God.

The First Commandment

Let's think for a moment about the First Commandment: "Thou shalt have no other gods before me" (Exodus 20:3 KJV). Does the way that we think of food or respond to opportunities to eat function as a god for us? Remember, an idol is anything that replaces God in our affections and worship. As a result, food, in a sense, has become our god: satisfying us, reassuring us, pleasing us.[4]

The Sixth Commandment

These practices are sinful because they harm the body, and the Sixth Commandment forbids this. It seems to me that this commandment, "Thou shalt not commit murder," is much broader than I have commonly thought of it. As I said in chapter 6, the commandment includes the idea of our seeking to *"preserve the life of ourselves* and others by resisting all . . . practices, which tend to the unjust taking away of life of any . . . *a sober use of meat, drink. . . ."*[5]

Since this may be a new concept for you, let me try to illustrate my point by referring to a different negative behavior: smoking. Given the scientific information now available on smoking, we can easily see how the habitual use of tobacco is a violation of the command to preserve our own lives. We know that if we consistently use tobacco we will greatly increase the possibility that we will develop mouth, throat, or lung cancer; emphysema; or heart disease. It is true that there are no implicit bans on tobacco in Scripture and that not everyone who smokes dies from it, but that doesn't negate the facts about the harm in using tobacco. It seems fairly obvious to me that habitual smoking violates the Sixth Commandment by slowly destroying the life that God has granted.

In the same way, I believe that if we consistently overeat, eat foods that do not nourish us or promote good health, cause ourselves to vomit or take excessive amounts of laxatives, overexercise, or starve ourselves, we are breaking this command. We are to protect, nourish, and care for our bodies. This is something that we may or may not already know how to do. Some of us may need to be taught by nutritionists how to eat properly. We don't automatically know how to eat what is best for us simply because our thoughts are often inaccurate and our desires are frequently sinful. We must let this command, "Thou shalt not murder," rule our food choices and help us determine whom we should listen to for counsel on eating. If, for instance, someone tells me that I can lose weight by eating only grapefruit and eggs, I have to ask myself if this will promote good health or not. I'm not a nutritionist, but I do know that there are guidelines developed by nutritionists about the most healthful ways of eating. Wisdom dictates that I listen to their counsel until they are proven wrong and seek to protect my health as best I can.

Implied Commands

Please bear with me as I try to make myself perfectly clear: I know that in the New Testament, there are no implicit commands regarding what foods may be eaten.[6] There are, however, a number of implied and indirect commands that we can follow to help guide our choices. We'll look at 12 of those commands in chapter 8, but let me get your thinking started here by asking a simple question:

Are Brownies Sinful?

You might be wondering if I think that you must repent if you eat a brownie. Well, the answer is both yes and no. You only need to repent when you eat a brownie if, for you to do so, is sin. If you know that you are enslaved to your appetites and that eating the brownie will bring you back under bondage, or feed wrongful desires for pleasure or control; or if you know that eating that much sugar all at once will send you into a binge; or if you believe that eating a brownie is somehow wrong (even if the Bible doesn't teach that it is), *then you must not eat it.* If you go ahead and compromise your conscience, you will be sinning. That is the direct and clear teaching of Scripture: "He who doubts is condemned if he eats, because his eating is not from faith; *and whatever is not from faith is sin*" (Romans 14:23, emphasis added). I know that this passage is speaking primarily about food offered to idols, but the principle remains: *Faithless eating is always sinful.* In fact, doing *anything* that compromises your faith is sin.

Does this help you to see why certain eating habits may be sinful? Let's just take a few more moments to examine the word *gluttony* and the way that it is used in Scripture.

Once again, I'm not trying to be offensive by using that word. It's humiliating for me to have to admit that I have succumbed to gluttony. I'm not name-calling here. Rather, I'm desiring to know what God thinks of my habits and how He tells me to change. I long to please Him, and the only way that I can do that is to think about my sin the way that He thinks of it. And that starts with calling it what He calls it.

Let's think about the word *gluttony* itself. *Gluttony* is defined as "habitual greed or excess in eating."[7] We don't hear much about gluttony these days; in fact, I don't think I've ever heard a sermon that spoke against gluttony. Because we never (or almost never) hear about gluttony being sinful, we had better take time to really examine this sin and understand what it involves.

What the Bible Teaches About Gluttony

In the Old Testament

It's interesting to note the context in which the word *gluttony* appears in the Old Testament. In Deuteronomy 21:18-20 we read:

> If any man has a stubborn and rebellious son who will not obey his father or his mother, and when they chastise him, he will not even listen to them, then his father and mother shall seize him, and bring him out to the elders of his city at the gateway of his home town. And they shall say to the elders of his city, "This son of ours is stubborn and rebellious, he will not obey us, he is a glutton and a drunkard."

Later, in Proverbs 23:20-21, we find this:

> Do not be with heavy drinkers of wine, or with gluttonous eaters of meat; for the heavy drinker and

the glutton will come to poverty, and drowsiness
will clothe a man with rags.

What can we learn from those two passages about gluttony? In the first passage, the disobedient son's sin was
accompanied by other sins: stubbornness, rebelliousness,
and drunkenness. Likewise, in Proverbs, we see gluttonous
eating connected with other forms of self-indulgence,
including drunkenness and laziness. One other important
fact we can infer from Proverbs is that self-indulgence is a
learned behavior—the wise son was warned about associ-
ating with gluttons lest he learn their ways.

In the New Testament

There is only one mention of gluttony in the New
Testament, which appears in Luke chapter 7. There we see
Jesus confronting His enemies. On the one hand they had
criticized John the Baptist for his asceticism, and on the
other they were criticizing Christ's liberty. Jesus responded:
"The Son of Man has come eating and drinking; and you
say, 'Behold, a gluttonous man, and a drunkard, a friend of
tax-gatherers and sinners!'" (Luke 7:34).

Jesus enjoyed being with people—He ate in the homes
of both the religious leaders and those who were considered the scum of the earth. He ate and He drank, but He
never gave Himself to the sins of gluttony and drunkenness.
Even though the Pharisees accused Him of being a gluttonous man and a drunkard, they were wrong. We know that
our Lord was sinless—He always did what was pleasing to
His Father.[8]

Not only was Jesus comfortable with eating and drinking, He also knew what it was to fast. Remember how He
went 40 days in the wilderness without food?[9] He didn't
ignore His appetite, however, and on at least two different
occasions He was concerned about His followers not
having enough food and performed miracles of multiplying

food so that they wouldn't go hungry and suffer harm.[10] He taught His disciples not to be worried about food because life was, after all, more than food.[11] He instituted the most important of Christian observances, communion, and used food (bread and wine) as ways to remind His children of His death and eventual return. Even after the resurrection, He cooked a breakfast of fish and bread on the beach with His disciples.[12] No, Jesus wasn't a glutton, but neither did He shy away from food or think that it was bad.

The apostle Paul echoed this same perspective in his letter to Timothy. He warned Timothy about false teachers, those who taught "doctrines of demons . . . men who . . . advocate abstaining from foods, which God has created to be gratefully shared in by those who believe and know the truth. For everything created by God is good, and nothing is to be rejected, if it is received with gratitude; for it is sanctified by means of the word of God and prayer" (1 Timothy 4:1, 3-5).

Paul taught that food was created by God and that it is to be gratefully shared in by believers. He knew that all of God's creation was good, and since this creation includes food, we are not to reject anything as being evil in and of itself. Let me expand on this: Bananas are not intrinsically wicked. (Bad banana! Isn't that a silly thought?) Even eating a banana is not wicked. In what case would it be sinful for me to eat a banana? When to do so would be gluttonous or faithless. It would also be sinful for me to eat a banana if I were not grateful for it and did not ask God's blessing on it. Paul teaches that we are to receive all food with grateful hearts and pray that God would use it for our benefit. If you can't honestly, with a pure heart, thank God for the food you are eating, then you shouldn't eat it. If you are just stuffing it down without a thought for God's good provision—if you are turning your nose up at something that He has laid before you—you are sinning.

Defining Gluttony

Biblically the word *glutton* means "a person who is debased and excessive in his eating habits. Gluttony is more than overeating. In its association with drunkenness, it describes a life given to excess."[13]

Do you see the pattern developing here? The sin doesn't merely lie in the fact that one might have too many potato chips. Rather, the sin lies in the fact that one's life is not self-disciplined—he lives a life of excess. He is living solely for himself. Allowing ourselves to have whatever we want, in whatever quantity we want, whenever we want it will lead to excess and the slavery of gluttony. Think about it as the difference between having a glass of wine with dinner and getting drunk. Gluttony is similar to getting drunk on food. Eating and eating, being unaware of what's going in your mouth, not tasting it, just stuffing it down till it makes you feel sick, till you appease all your desires, and doing this over and over, making it a habit—that's gluttony.

Gluttony Portrayed

The popular English thinker and writer C.S. Lewis describes a different form of gluttony in his insightful little book *The Screwtape Letters.* This book is written in the form of ongoing correspondence written from one demon to another on the methods of temptation. In the following excerpt, Screwtape is instructing his nephew Wormwood on the benefits of entrapping people in the sin of gluttony:

> One of the great achievements of the last hundred years has been to deaden the human conscience on [the subject of gluttony]. This has largely been effected by concentrating all our efforts on gluttony of Delicacy, not gluttony of Excess. Your patient's mother . . . would be astonished . . . to learn that *her whole life is enslaved to this kind of sensuality*, which is quite concealed

from her by the fact that the quantities involved are small. *But what do quantities matter, provided we can use a human belly and palate to produce queru-lousness (complaining), impatience, uncharitable-ness, and self-concern?* . . . This woman is a positive terror to hostesses and servants. Because what she wants is smaller and less costly than what has been set before her, she never recognizes as gluttony her determination to *get what she wants*, no matter how troublesome it may be to others. The real value of the . . . work . . . can be gauged by the way in which her belly now *dominates her whole life* . . . her *greed* has been one of the chief sources of [her son's] discomfort for many years (emphasis added).[14]

As long as what you eat dominates your affections, thoughts, and behavior—even if you are eating small portions, starving yourself, or insisting on eating only "healthy" foods—your eating is gluttonous because your life is focused on food.

We can learn to judge if we are being gluttonous by the way that we respond to others when we don't get what we want to eat. Are we rude to the waiter who messes up our order? Do we snap at our husband for taking so long to get home before dinner? Do we position ourselves to grab the juiciest piece of chicken before the kids? (What do they care?) Do we scream at our parents when they ask us to come to the table and eat? Such bitter water flowing from our life may well indicate that we have become enslaved to our appetites.

Thin Gluttons

By the way, it's not just overweight people who are guilty of the sin of gluttony. It's possible for a person's weight prob-lems to have causes not related to gluttonous eating. There are many thin people who are ruled by their appetites as well. Perhaps they are thin because they starve themselves; perhaps they are thin because they purge; perhaps they are thin because they have one of those supersonic metabolisms. So a person's weight should not be used to measure whether gluttony is in the picture. And remember, losing weight isn't the measure of success. The measure is your heart and the streams that flow from it. Only you can answer the question of whether you are gluttonous or not.

Unfortunately, it's usually only those who have a weight problem who realize they need to confront their gluttony. We need to examine our attitude toward food no matter what our weight is. And ultimately, we can rejoice that God does use our concerns about our looks as a means to attack gluttony.

An Invitation to Change

What are your thoughts about your eating patterns in view of what we've just learned from Scripture? Are you already coming up with ideas for changes you'd like to make? My hope is that so far this chapter has given you some idea of how God may view your eating habits and how you need to be sensitive to how you handle this area of your life. Chances are that you see some ways in which you'd like to bring change because you want to eat in a way that glorifies God, which means doing away with any habits that are sinful.

Understanding Habits

Because our eating patterns are pretty much established by habit, we'll find it helpful to understand how habits function.

Habits are a wonderful gift from God. It is only because I have a habit of typing that I can sit in front of my computer and get any work done at all. If I had to think before every key stroke—*find the "a," press the key, find the "b"*... I would never get anything done! God gave us habits so that we wouldn't have to find it necessary to keep relearning the common, mundane functions of our daily lives. He freed us from the slavery of having to think, *How do I tie my shoe? How do I drive my car?* What's more, we have a wonderful capacity to establish new habits—sometimes without really trying. Just do something 4 or 5 times in a row and—presto!—you're beginning to establish a habit.

Because we have this wonderful capacity to form habits, we can be encouraged that we can change. Even though you may presently have habits that trouble you, cheer yourself with the knowledge that, at the least, you are able to form new habits. Stop now and think about any habit that you have, even if it's sinful. If you are able to establish *any* habit, even if it's a sinful one, you *can* develop godly ones. It may be difficult—I have no doubt that it will be—but remember that the power of all of heaven is on your side.

Whenever I think about trying to break an old habit, I feel myself getting fearful and anxious. I don't like breaking my old habits (or learning new ones) because the old ones are so comfortable. I might not feel happy about my ungodly habits (indeed I don't), but at least I know them and they seem to fit nicely into my life. And it's only when I've decided that my habit is sinful and that I must change it that I have the power to actually do so. Saying no to a cozy old friend is difficult, but I am able to do so because I have the power of the Holy Spirit working in me. It's because of His power that you and I became new creatures in Christ, and it will be because of His power that we'll be transformed in the future.

Dr. Jay Adams provides these helpful thoughts about the ongoing struggle to break old sinful habits:

> . . . desires of sin, habituated in the body by years of service to sin, will be to do unrighteousness. So sin must no longer be obeyed. Its *desires*

> (that over time have become habitual desires of the body) will tend in the wrong direction. Your body (which includes the brain, programmed by your sinful nature) will desire to do sinful things that you know you must not do. So you both desire and do not desire to do them. [You love and hate to eat.][15]

We all have many habits, and the warfare that we are involved in between our desire to serve our old habits and our desire to serve God is a struggle all Christians face. Even the great apostle Paul was familiar with this struggle.[16] His heart yearned for the Christians at Rome to break their old sinful habits by replacing them with new, godly ones:

> Do not let sin reign in your mortal body that you should obey its lusts, and do not go on presenting the members of your body to sin as instruments of unrighteousness; but present yourselves to God as those alive from the dead, and your members as instruments of righteousness to God (Romans 6:12-13).

Let's take a few moments to try to understand just what Paul meant when he told his friends, the Christians at Rome, to stop presenting their bodies to sin as instruments of unrighteousness.

Weapons of Righteousness

We are involved in a warfare between righteousness and unrighteousness, God's way of living and Satan's way, self-control and wrong eating patterns. Paul teaches that we must stop employing the parts of our body—our hands, our mouth, our eyes—as instruments or "weapons" of sin. When we allow ourselves to use the parts of our body to sin, we are, in effect, aiding our enemy by giving him weapons to use against our soul. Why would we want to aid our enemy? Can you imagine giving a gun to someone who is trying to rob you? That is the picture that Paul is painting in this verse. Giving any part of our body over to fulfill our sinful desires is the same as helping our enemy hurt us.

Our habitual desires are strong, but we have God's promise that if we determine to fight temptation, we will be victorious: "Resist the devil and he will flee from you" (James 4:7). Look at your hands. God made them and then He purchased them by the sacrifice of His Son. Tell yourself, "These are holy hands. I'm not going to use them for my enemy's work any longer." Go to your mirror and look at your mouth. Say, "This mouth is holy. I'm not going to use it for my enemy's work any longer." As you grow in this determination, you will find that your habitual sin will become weaker and weaker.

"But," you may be thinking, "what if my habitual sin is too strong? I've been doing this for so long, and I've tried and tried to change." Paul answers this question in Romans 6:14: "Sin shall not be master over you, for you are not under law, but under grace." Read that verse again. Are you rejoicing in this promise? If it were up to you and me—if we didn't have God's strengthening power, His grace—we would never be able to make a statement like that. As you determine to put off your old habits and, by His grace, put on new habits, you will be able to say with Paul, "Sin will not be master over me." Say that to yourself . . . "Sin will not be master over me." When your hands are tempted to reach for more food than you need, say, "Sin will not be master over me." When your mouth longs for something sweet and you know you're already full, say, "Sin will not be master over me." When you find yourself fearful and consumed with thinking about food, say, "Sin will not be master over me." You can be victorious over your wrong habits, even though it will be a battle, because you're determining not to give the enemy any weapons to use against you. Every part of your body—your hands, your mouth, your tongue, your stomach—is His, and by His power you're going to change.

I'll leave the rest of this discussion to the next chapter because the only way to successfully put off one habit is by putting something in its place, and that's what is involved in step two. I've learned that it isn't enough just to tell myself to stop performing some wrong habit. No, I have to learn how to replace my ungodly habit with a godly one, and that's what we'll look at next.

A Real Freedom

For now, though, let me encourage you to spend a few moments in prayer. Pray that God will give you the grace to say, "Sin will not be master over me" with faith and the assurance that this is God's plan for you. You may be facing a real battle now, but God has already committed all of the resources of heaven to free you from sin. You can smile as you pray, "Sin will not be master over me." You can do this because you already have a Master, and He's strong enough and loving enough to free you from any bondage to old habits you might have. Insert your name into this prayer, just as I've done with my name: "Lord, I'm believing right now that sin will not be master over *Elyse*—because of Your power, because of Your goodness, because of Your never-ending love. Sin *will not* be master over me. I know that on my own I could never accomplish this. But because You are who You are, I know that sin will not be master over *me*."

8

MAKING GODLY FOOD CHOICES

"...and having been freed from sin,
you became slaves of righteousness...."

—ROMANS 6:18

e covered a lot of ground in our last chapter, didn't we? And I'm sure that you're anxious to move on . . . eager to take note of practical ways to bring real and lasting change. That's what we're going to begin doing right now—in the upcoming pages, I'm going to outline what I believe godly eating consists of and how you can begin today to practice it. That brings us to the second step in the process of change:

Step Two: Become convinced that God's
methods for disciplined eating are right
and begin practicing them.

Together we have come to recognize that no food is, in itself, sinful. However, in a number of ways, it's possible for certain foods or specific eating habits to be sinful. At first glance, it may appear that the Bible does not have much to say in the way of practical insights about our eating habits. However, when God gave us the Bible, He didn't try to cover every minute aspect of life. Rather, He gave us general principles that would apply to the incredible range of issues we face each day. And sure enough, He gave us an extremely practical principle that's applicable to every aspect of our eating habits. This is the principle of self-control, or self-discipline.

The Results of the Spirit's Work

In the book of Galatians,[1] Paul outlines a number of character traits. Some represent the work of our flesh, and the others represent the fruit of the Spirit's work in our life. One of the qualities that demonstrates that the Spirit has been at work in a believer's life is self-control. In the original Greek text, this word can be translated "self-discipline," "self-control," or "temperance." Since temperance has come to mean self-control in one specific area, the consumption of alcohol, this word isn't as inclusive for us as the New Testament means for it to be.

The word translated "self-control" in the New Testament means "control over sensual desires. It indicates a self-control that masters all kinds of sensual desires. Through [it] the Christian disciplines body and spirit, so that he is more capable of striving for his spiritual reward."[2]

Paul uses the term in reference to the way that he treated his own body:

> Everyone who competes in the games exercises self-control in all things. They then do it to receive a perishable wreath, but we an imperishable. Therefore I run in such a way, as not without aim; I box in such a way, as not beating the air; but I buffet my body and make it my slave, lest possibly, after I

have preached to others, I myself should be disqualified (1 Corinthians 9:25-27).

Look again at the verbs that Paul employs to depict his struggle against his bodily desires. He *exercises* self-control, *runs* and *fights* purposefully, he *buffets* and *enslaves* his body to his desire to gain the imperishable reward of God's pleasure. These are not little sissy terms that he is using. The word "buffet" in verse 27 is a fighting term. It means to "hit under the eye" or to disable an enemy—to habitually deal knockout blows to one's appetites! Furthermore, when Paul says that he makes his body his slave, he means that he is a slave-driver over the passions of his own body!

Paul would never have counseled anyone to eat anything that he or she wanted, even if the amounts were not excessive. No, Paul had a different view of the appetites of the body. He saw them as a doorway to disqualification. He was an athlete training for a goal. Just like an athlete, he pushed himself and restricted his activities. "No," he says, "if you want to eat that food, you can, but I'm in training. I'm afraid that if I eat that food with you, I'll be too sluggish and too enamored with this world and my comforts here to keep my eye on the goal. I'll start thinking that my goal is to please myself and then I'll be lost. After all my training, after I've trained so many others, I might be disqualified from the races right before it's time for me to run."

Earning God's Acceptance?

Paul paints an interesting picture, doesn't he? It's not that controlling your eating earns you anything (as to your standing) before God. That's what Paul meant when he said elsewhere: "Food will not commend us to God; we are neither the worse if we do not eat, nor the better if we do eat" (1 Corinthians 8:8). Sometimes Christians think that striving to be obedient in their eating is legalistic. That's because they are confused about the place of obedience in a Christian's life. Sometimes they feel that striving to be obedient might negate the wonderful gift of salvation and because they love the Lord and don't want to offend Him, they shrink back from attempting to live a disciplined life.

Let me try to clear up this confusion because in one sense, these Christians are right to be concerned. If we are trying to *merit* God's love or *earn* His grace by living a disciplined life, then we are wrong. Our standing before God is accomplished solely by His unmerited favor whereby He applies the perfect righteousness of Christ to the account of completely undeserving and helpless sinners. This activity is called *justification*. When it comes to your justification, you can't add one thing. You could eat in a self-controlled manner for the rest of your life and never earn anything but judgment. It is Christ's righteousness *plus nothing* that pays the debt of your sin. If you are a Christian, your justification has been accomplished. You don't have to work on it—in fact, there's nothing you could do to enhance it in anyway.

Sanctification, on the other hand, is different. Sanctification, the process of change that we've been discussing in this book, is *active*. It's the process of your becoming righteous like Christ in your *lifestyle*, and it's a work of the Spirit that you are to be actively involved in. This change may be very slow—certainly you will not have immediate perfection, but you are now responsible and enabled to obey your new Master. You are responsible to put off your old sinful habits and enabled to put on new godly ones by the power of the Holy Spirit. Self-control is one of the keys in this process.

The Need for Self-Control

Paul believed that self-control was so important that when he had opportunity to witness to a very important ruler, it was one of the three main topics he spoke about.[3] But Paul wasn't the only one who talked about it. Peter also wrote about self-control and said that it helps us to avoid becoming useless and unfruitful. He wrote that Christians are to strive diligently to grow in moral excellence, knowledge, *self-control*, perseverance, godliness, brotherly kindness and love (2 Peter 1:5-7). All of these virtues are intertwined and are necessary for your usefulness and fruitfulness to Christ. Growing in these qualities is so important that "he who lacks these qualities is blind or short-sighted, having forgotten his purification from his former sins" (2 Peter 1:9). Lack of self-control blinds us to the realities of the temporary nature of this earth's pleasures and our own sinfulness, and hardens our hearts to the joys and purposes of heaven. This thought is reiterated in the Bible's lists of qualifications for spiritual leadership—practically every list mentions self-control as a prerequisite.

Young Daniel, captive in Babylon and soon to be leader of his people, also practiced self-control—even at the peril of his life. For some reason, probably because of Jewish dietary laws, Daniel believed that it would defile him to eat the "king's choice food," so he requested and received permission to eat only vegetables.[4] This was a difficult stand for him to take because to refuse the king's food was not allowed. But God protected Daniel, who, because of his stand, was blessed with health and greater strength than the captives who ate the king's food.

Guidelines for Self-Controlled Eating

So, how can we be self-controlled in our eating? Does that mean that we should eat a only certain number of calories, avoid sugar, eliminate foods with fat, or perhaps a combination of all three?

The easiest thing in the world for me to do would be to tell you exactly what you should eat. I could tell you that if you cut out all sugar from your diet, you'll be cured! But that's a rather simplistic approach that doesn't take into consideration a wide variety of factors. Besides, chances are you have been on diets like that before, and you and I both know how they usually end. I'm not saying that it is wrong to follow a preplanned diet, as long as it is not a fad diet—such as eating nothing but grapefruit and eggs for two weeks. In fact, for many women, I strongly encourage a preplanned diet. *But even if you are following a preplanned diet perfectly, that doesn't mean that your eating is pleasing to the Lord.* I can lust over a cup of nonfat frozen yogurt in exactly the same way that I can over a chocolate shake. I can also become enamored with my appearance and worry that I might gain weight, which wouldn't please God. No, there are other criteria for you and me to consider as we develop our personal plan for disciplined eating. As we consider these criteria, remember that there is no magic bullet that can help us to achieve instant success.

Over the next few pages I have listed 12 questions you can ask yourself in order to determine whether your eating is sinful or not. To help you remember these points, I've developed the acrostic "D-I-S-C-I-P-L-I-N-E-D Eating." You'll want to memorize this acrostic so that you can get in the habit of thinking about it regularly.

As you consider the following, some of the answers will be obvious. Others will take some time and careful thought. Stop now and prayerfully ask God to help you as you think about how to make your eating habits more pleasing to Him.

1. **D**oubt: *Do I doubt (for whatever reason) that I can eat this food without sinning?* Once again, it may not be sinful for you to eat a brownie *per se*, but if you believe that it is sin for you to do so, you must not do it. Now, you can seek to grow in your understanding of Scripture and strengthen your conscience, but until you can sincerely say, "This isn't sinful for me any longer," you had better abstain. The apostle Paul affirms this in Romans 14:23, where he said, "He who doubts is condemned if he eats, because his eating

is not from faith; and whatever is not from faith is sin."

2. **I**dolatry: *Does eating this particular food demonstrate a heart* either of independence—"I can do whatever I want"—or a heart longing for pleasure—"I know that I don't need this for my sustenance, but I love the feeling of the sweet coldness"? It is important to ask yourself whether you are eating because you're hungry and you need nourishment or if you are eating for reasons that, ultimately, are idolatrous. We've talked a lot about idols, but let me remind you that an idol is anything (inherently good or evil) that draws your affections away from God. You can judge whether you're worshiping an idol if you are willing to sin (in any way) to serve it. You can also judge whether you are worshiping an idol by observing the streams that flow from your life when you are pursuing your desire. For instance, if you are damaging your health or acting in ungodly ways (such as spending too much money, being irritable or unkind, seeking your own will), then you are probably serving another god. Remember that the first and foremost command of all is, "You shall have no other gods before Me" (Exodus 20:3).

3. **S**tumble: *If I eat this, will it cause a weaker Christian to stumble?* For instance, if I know that my friend will go on a binge or compromise her beliefs if I give her a piece of candy, or even eat one in front of her, then I should not do so. It's not that you should have an oversensitive conscience, saying that a piece of candy is sinful for you. No, the sin would come from the fact that you don't love your sister enough to forgo what, for you, is legitimate so that she won't sin. "It is good not to eat meat or to drink wine, or to do

anything by which your brother stumbles" (Romans 14:21).

4. Coveting: *Am I eating this just because I saw someone else with it and I'm coveting it?* This is one place where TV commercials—especially those for fast food—cause many people to sin. These commercials are written expressly to cause you to covet what you see someone eating. Don't forget—your eyes are a powerful channel for temptation. Observe the way that Eve was tempted in the Garden of Eden: "When the woman *saw* that the tree was good for food, and that it was *a delight to the eyes*, and that the tree was desirable to make one wise, she took from its fruit and ate" (Genesis 3:6, emphasis added). She saw the fruit; she thought it looked good; she ate it. Satan is still operating in the same way today. The media is a convenient tool for stirring up discontent with our own circumstances. Discontent springs out of a heart that is coveting what someone else has. Scripture, however, says "You shall not covet . . . anything that belongs to your neighbor" (Exodus 20:17).

5. Inroad: *If I eat this, will it create an inroad for sin?* For instance, I know that whenever I eat chocolate it opens a door for me to desire more and more and I end up eating a lot of candy over a number of days—much more than I should for good health. Chocolate also contains caffeine, which I've eliminated from my diet. So, because of my weakness in this area, and for the sake of better health, it is best if I abstain from chocolate altogether. Since there is no command to eat chocolate, and I don't have to have it to maintain health or to demonstrate thankfulness for God's provision, I can abstain in good conscience.

Here are some additional scenarios: Is there any particular restaurant that you frequent where you spend more money than is prudent, eat too much food, or where you are usually very demanding with the staff? If you make that bowl of popcorn, will you then sit down in front of the television and waste time? If you eat one chip, will it create a desire in you to overindulge in chips or other salty, oily foods? Even if it isn't sinful for you to eat a particular food, or even if that food is not prohibited by your diet, you shouldn't eat it if it is a door to other sins. Rather, "put on the Lord Jesus Christ, and make no provision for the flesh in regard to its lusts" (Romans 13:14).

6. Praise: *Can I eat this food with thanks and gratitude? Is my heart overflowing with songs of praise to Him?* Can I eat this with a truly thankful heart, or will I be eating in the face of God, with an attitude that says, "I'm going to eat this even though I know that it's wrong! I don't care about You and Your commands! You aren't giving me what I want, so I'll just eat this (or starve myself)." If you are unable to sincerely thank God for what you are about to eat, then you shouldn't eat it.

On the other hand, we must not exercise such scruples that we turn our noses up at what God has called "good"—the food that He has created. God's creation is to be used and enjoyed by His children, and when we receive it with thankful prayer and with minds that are informed by Scripture, He blesses it to us and nourishes us by it. Consider how the psalmist describes the Lord's delight in giving you food to eat: "He causes the grass to grow for the cattle, and vegetation for the labor of man, so that he may bring forth food from the earth, and wine which makes man's heart glad, so that he may make his face glisten with oil, and food which sustains man's heart" (Psalm 104:14-15). This is a particularly important point for those who look at food as being bad or evil. "For everything created by God is good, and nothing is to be rejected, if it is received with gratitude" (1 Timothy 4:4).

7. Life: *Would eating this food harm my health in any way?* For instance, eating prime rib when I have high cholesterol; eating too much sugar if I have blood sugar problems (i.e., hypoglycemia or diabetes); eating high-calorie food or too much low-calorie food even though I am obese; and starving myself, abusing laxatives, or overexercising are all practices that will lessen my strength to do God's work and will decrease the quality of my life.

God holds your life's span in His hand, but you must not be presumptuous with Him and say, "Oh well, God will take care of me." It is true that God cares for His children, but He also gives you intelligence that you must use as well. Each person must eat what, for him or her, is a healthy diet. For some, this might mean frequenting the health food store and taking herbs and eating all-natural food. For others, this might mean being more careful about avoiding foods high in fat or calories, or adhering to eating nutritionally balanced diets. The decision is yours, and you just want to make sure that you're not compromising your personal belief system or conscience. Remember, God has given you a grave responsibility to care for your body; for you to do otherwise is sinful. "Thou shalt not murder" (Exodus 20:13 KJV).

8. Illustrate: *Am I modeling good eating habits for others and encouraging them to be self-disciplined, or do I encourage others to self-indulge? Am I illustrat-ing what it means to be a temperate, joyful, free*

believer? What kinds of behaviors am I teaching my
fellow family members? Do I tell them to serve God
with all their heart and then show them that I serve
food instead? People are watching, and although it's
wrong to impress others so that they will think you're
great, it's not wrong to be careful about maintaining
a godly lifestyle for the sake of our witness to others:
". . . show yourself an illustration of those who
believe" (1 Timothy 4:12).

9. **N**o: *Am I able to say no to this even if I know that I
   can eat it without sin?* From time to time it's beneficial just to say no to your desires even if you are
   physically hungry for some particular food. This is
   one place where proper fasting comes in. I must
   keep reminding myself that satisfying every whim of
   my body is self-serving, even if I do have Christian
   liberty. I relish my liberty in Christ, but I must keep
   my bodily desires in submission to my heart's desire
   to please God. "I buffet my body and make it my
   slave, lest possibly, after I have preached to others, I
   myself should be disqualified" (1 Corinthians 9:27).

10. **E**motions: *Does the desire to eat this flow out of a
    heart of anger, fear, frustration, or depression?* Anger
    says, "I'll show you . . . I'll eat this candy bar and
    you'll be sorry!" Fear says, "I may never have the
    opportunity to eat this again!" or "I might not be
    strong enough to do everything I have to do."
    Frustration says, "I worked hard today and I deserve
    this!" And depression says, "I'm so bummed out, I'm
    just going to eat this—who cares anyway?" If you give
    in to the desire to eat because you are sinfully angry,
    fearful, worried, frustrated, or depressed, that sin will
    end up taking mastery of you. "If you do well, will not
    your countenance be lifted up? And if you do not do

well, sin is crouching at the door; and its desire is for you, but you must master it" (Genesis 4:7).

11. **D**istract: *Will preparing or eating this food distract me from something better that God has for me to do?* For instance, would I do better by ministering to the Lord or my guests rather than spending excessive amounts of time cooking some elaborate meal and being frustrated that others aren't as impressed about my cooking as I am? (Does it really matter if the gravy is lumpy? Will anyone remember that you spent hours cooking, or will they remember that you loved them and spent time ministering to them in conversation, prayer, and fellowship?) Will I sin by going out to lunch and being more concerned that the waiter gets my order right and then so relishing the eating of the food that I ignore the fact that there is someone across the table to whom I could minister?

I'm sure you know about Lazarus' sisters, Martha and Mary. Martha had a problem with distraction. She was busy preparing a meal for Jesus, who was their guest, and she was frustrated that Mary was sitting at Jesus' feet rather than helping her. She complained to the Lord and He put the whole thing in perspective: "Martha, Martha, you are worried and bothered about so many things; but only a few things are necessary, really only one, for Mary has chosen the good part, which shall not be taken away from her" (Luke 10:41-42).

12. **E**nslaved: *Does it bring me under any kind of bondage?* For instance, caffeine has a powerfully enslaving effect and you may need to question whether it is right for you to bring yourself under its bondage. What would happen to your Christian witness if you didn't get your shot in the morning? Would you continue to be filled with thanksgiving

and praise? There are other things that can enslave us, such as donuts every morning or popcorn every night. In fact, almost anything can enslave us. If we find that we just *have* to have such-and-such every day, that would be a good time to practice abstinence until you know that you have mastered this desire. If you practice habits of bulimia, you must ask yourself whether this food is something that has habitually led to a binge. If you battle anorexia, you will need to ask whether eating this will entice you to starve yourself or overexercise tomorrow. You may have the Christian liberty to eat this food, but is it profitable? Will you be mastered by it? "All things are lawful for me, but not all things are profitable. All things are lawful for me, but I will not be mastered by anything" (1 Corinthians 6:12).

You may be thinking there's no way that you'll be able remember all these words. But if you ask for God's help and start right now, you can do it. Start now by writing out the letters D-I-S-C-I-P-L-I-N-E-D Eating in the space below and see how many you can guess correctly. (I've done the first one for you).

With consistent effort, in little time I'm sure you'll be able to remember the word. Once you remember the words, you could also memorize the Scripture verses that accompany each one. Then, when you are tempted to eat sinfully, you can fight the temptation with Scripture, just as Jesus did.[5] Each of these verses (with their corresponding questions) are written out in Appendix B so you can copy them and keep them with you.

D __ __ __ __ __ __ __ __ __ __ __ __
o
u
b
t

All of this, of course, can be summed up by one question:

> *In my eating and drinking, am I glorifying God?*
> (1 Corinthians 10:31).

Additional Considerations

An Eating Program

If you are significantly over- or underweight, you may need to monitor the number of calories you are eating so you can attain better health. It is best to do this with the help of a dietician or physician. But there are numbers of good, well-balanced diets that you can go on that will act as a model for you as you learn to eat in a more disciplined fashion. The American Heart Association[6] or The American Diabetes Association[7] diets are both excellent and will promote good health and new habits.

Your Daily Allotment of Calories

If you are seeking to lose weight, and you need help determining how many calories you might want to eat, then multiply your healthy goal weight by 9-10 (for women) or 11-13 (for men). For instance, if a healthy weight for you is approximately 150 pounds, you can multiply that by 9 (9 x 150), which equals 1350. This is the total number of calories you can eat to maintain (or achieve) a weight of 150. If you consistently, over a long period of time, eat 1350 calories per day, you will probably continue to lose weight until you reach your goal.[8]

Let's assume that the number of calories you should eat on a daily basis is 1350. You can take 1200 of these calories and divide them up between the three most calorie-rich food sources: Carbohydrates, proteins, and fat. Of these, you should spend no more than 60 percent (or 720 calories) on carbohydrates, which include breads, starches, pastas, and cereals. Fifteen percent of your calories (180) should be allotted to proteins, which would include all meats and soybean products. (Remember that high-fat meats have more calories, so you'll have to eat smaller portions of them to stay within your percentages.) Fat, which includes butter, margarine, salad dressings, and animal and vegetable oils, should account for no more than 25 percent, or 300 calories. You can split the remaining 150 calories between dairy products, fruits, and vegetables (which are generally very low in calories). This formula is very simplistic, however, and doesn't take into account people's differences in body mass (fat/muscle mass) or the amount of exercise you're doing. Your physician or nutritionist would be the best resource for you to consult as you endeavor to set up a healthy eating program.

A Specific Diet?

If the advice that I've just given isn't enough for you to get going with your disciplined eating, then you might need the help of a specific eating plan. Some of us do better with detailed strategies, while others of us know enough about how to eat properly that we really don't need anyone to tell us. You make the decision. And remember that you can always change your mind. If you discover that you can't stay focused without a specific diet, then go ahead and use one. If, on the other hand, you find yourself ignoring the D-I-S-C-I-P-L-I-N-E-D Eating criteria and falling back into habits of following a diet without thinking about God's perspective, then you might have to concentrate on the questions asked by the acronym for a time. Remember, this is a process—try to be patient and get settled in for the long haul. The change will be more gratifying to you and will be truly pleasing to the Lord.

Since weight loss is not our primary goal, you need to resist the temptation to try to lose more than ½ - 1 pound per week. Beware of diets that promise quick weight loss, since most of this loss consists of water weight, and quick-loss regimens may also be damaging to your muscle mass. And remember: No fad diets! We don't need another fad diet that will feed our impatience and our vanity. We need to learn how to eat in a self-disciplined manner, even if that means that we will not have rapid weight loss.

Exercise

Since trained muscle is able to burn more fat, building up your muscle mass is a great way to improve your ability to lose weight. (Don't worry, you won't end up looking like Arnold Schwartzeneggar!) As we age, our resting metabolic rate (the rate that calories are burned at rest) goes down about 3 percent per decade. It is assumed this is so because of the loss of muscle mass that occurs with aging and a more sedentary lifestyle. That's why you could eat all those burgers when you were 19 and never gain an ounce . . . and that's why you may have gained some weight in the last few years. But don't despair! If you increase your muscle mass by doing resistance training three days a week, the number of calories that you'll burn (even when you're resting) can increase by 15 percent[9]—and that means you'll lose fat, trim down, and be more healthy sooner—even if you don't actually see a great drop in your weight.

You don't need to go to the gym to get resistance train-ing—lifting a big can of tomato soup, doing modified sit-ups (crunches), squats, and modified push-ups will help you begin to build and tone your muscles. If the gym isn't an option, why not check out some of those exercise videos? Whatever you choose to do, just remember that moderation is one of the keys to a successful fitness program.

A Daily Diary

I have found that it is helpful to keep a daily diary such as the sample one I've placed in Appendix C at the back of this book. Over a period of days, we frequently aren't aware of the specific amounts or kinds of food that we are eating, and while you're learning to ask yourself the D-I-S-C-I-P-L-I-N-E-D Eating questions habitually, keeping a daily diary will be an invaluable tool for you to use. This will help give you a good idea of the big picture of your eating habits.

Beginning today, you should use this diary to record *everything* that you eat. Even though your eating habits may not change immediately, you need to begin determining which areas of the D-I-S-C-I-P-L-I-N-E-D Eating criteria you have the most trouble with. You need to be very detailed about recording what you have eaten—indicating the approximate amount of food and, if you sinned in eating, the principle that you violated. So that you can see what a completed daily diary looks like, I've provided sample pages in Appendix D. As you keep track of your eating for a few days, you'll probably see certain patterns emerge. We all tend to sin in predictable, habitual ways, and it probably won't take you long to find your personal areas of weakness. These are the areas that you need to concentrate on and build walls against. We'll talk more about this in chapter 10, which is titled, "Practice, Practice, Practice."

If you decide to go on a specific diet, then be sure to record everything that the diet requires as well (fat grams or calories, for instance). At first this will seem cumbersome and time-consuming. Just remember, however, that God's work in you is slow but steady, and all you need to do is persevere diligently. You won't be able to grow in your understanding of God's way for you to eat without keeping track of your failures and victories. Let me gently encourage you not to be lazy about this. It will take effort on your part, but remember that God is working together with you. Take time now, if you haven't already, to acquaint yourself with the daily diary. Permission is granted for you to make copies of the daily diary for your personal use. Make the copies and write on them—don't write in the book or you won't be able to use the journal again later.

For at least the first month or so, you should review your daily diary every evening. You should look over the choices you made and review the D-I-S-C-I-P-L-I-N-E-D Eating questions. At the end of the week, look over your diary again. Circle any specific failures that occur more than three times. For instance, if *idolatry* shows up several times, and you see that you are very interested in pleasing yourself with sweets, then make it a goal to avoid these foods for a time as part of your quest to bring your body under subjection to your spirit. As we learned earlier, even though your particular eating plan may say that a certain food is allowable for you, that doesn't mean that you should eat it. An example of this would be overeating fat-free cookies because you are counting fat grams rather than calories.

The more you practice this discipline, the more you'll grow in your wisdom and understanding. You must also take time for prayer, confessing any sinful eating that you discover. Take time to praise God and rejoice in any victories that He has given you. Pray specifically that God will keep you from temptation, especially in those areas of personal weakness.

The Spiritual Disciplines

If you do not have a habit of reading your Bible and praying daily, you'll also want to keep track of these spiritual disciplines in your daily diary. You can do this by recording in your diary the chapters of the Bible which you read that day. (I recommend reading at least two chapters, but you can read as much as you like.) You'll want to record the time of day that you pray, since you are seeking to establish a regular habit. Try to pray at the same time every day. Remember to pray that God will convict you of sin, give you wisdom, and keep you from temptation.

Fasting

There's one more spiritual discipline I'd like to mention—one that we don't hear much about these days. I would like to recommend that you practice the spiritual discipline of fasting at least one meal a week, unless for you to do so would be sin (i.e., if you are already underweight, or if you know that a fast will throw you into a binge). There are many examples of fasting in Scripture, and it is has been a powerful tool in my life to humble me and free me from ungodly desires. I say that fasting humbles me because I have found out, very quickly, just how demanding my bodily appetites are. Fasting assists me in reminding my body that my spirit is in control, and that pleasing God is more important than satisfying my hunger. You should always fast with caution, however, and never fast from taking water. You can take the time that you normally would spend eating (lunch is a great meal to fast) and spend it in prayer instead. If you are unable to fast for whatever reason, then fast something besides food, such as television or recreational reading, for instance.

We'll explain more about these disciplines in chapter 10. For now, let me encourage you that you—yes, even you—can develop habits of D-I-S-C-I-P-L-I-N-E-D Eating. You can do this because it is God's plan for you to be sanctified, and each of these points are based on principles found in His Word. Why not spend some time in prayer right now, asking Him to write His truth on your heart?

9

FOOD AND YOUR THOUGHT LIFE

*"We are destroying speculations and every lofty thing raised
up against the knowledge of God, and we are taking every
thought captive to the obedience of Christ."*

—2 CORINTHIANS 10:5

*H*ow much do our eating habits reflect our thoughts? Jenny wondered about this in our Bible study class one evening. "Since we've been thinking about the D-I-S-C-I-P-L-I-N-E-D Eating acrostic, I've discovered that I think a lot about food. I daydream about what I'm going to have for lunch and then I daydream about what's for dinner. I think about what I'm going to eat, how it will taste, even where I'm going to sit when I eat it. I can make my mouth water by thinking about a BLT sandwich—in fact, I frequently do. And then, even though I have good intentions to eat properly at dinner, I find myself drawn to BLT sandwiches. Sometimes I find myself getting up in the middle of the night and making a sandwich. I love the taste of it, the smell of it—but then afterwards I hate the fact that I ate it. It's dawning on me that I need to control my thoughts, but how do I do this? In my mind I know what I should do, but how do I change my heart?"

The Bible has much to say about our thoughts. Our thoughts influence our behavior, our emotions, and even our health. As we examine step three of the change process more closely, we will need to look at what the Bible has to say about our thinking.

First, however, I believe it would be beneficial for us to clear up a common misunderstanding.

Thinking in Your Heart

In my counseling I have commonly heard women say what Jenny said: "I know in my mind what I should do, but how do I change my heart?" You might have heard someone say something like this before, or a similar statement that goes, "I have that knowledge in my head, but I need to get it into my heart." We know what the person means; he is saying that he believes the statement is true, but that he hasn't acted on it or felt that it was true. Perhaps he even meant that he had trouble obeying it. Whatever the case, people commonly talk about the difference between "heart knowledge" and "head knowledge." Although it seems plausible that there might be a differentiation like this, the Bible never mentions it. I don't want to belabor this point, but because I'm going to be talking about both thinking and feeling in this chapter, please bear with me.

Jesus, who knew the hearts and thoughts of all men, didn't see a division between the heart and mind. He demonstrated this by making statements like, "For out of the *heart* come evil *thoughts*" (Matthew 15:19) and, "Jesus, aware in His spirit that they were reasoning that way within themselves, said to them, 'Why are you *reasoning* about these things in your *hearts*?'" (Mark 2:8).

The writers of the New Testament didn't see this distinction between the heart and mind, either. "He has done mighty deeds with His arm; He has scattered those who were proud in the *thoughts* of their *heart*," says Luke 1:51. In Hebrews 4:12 we read, "The word of God is living and active and sharper than any two-edged sword . . . and able to judge the *thoughts and intentions of the heart*." And in the Old Testament, Moses wrote, "Then the LORD saw that the wickedness of man was great on the earth, and that every intent of the *thoughts of his heart* was only evil continually" (Genesis 6:5).

No, the Bible doesn't make any distinction between the head and the heart—and neither should we.

The Biblical Distinction

Simply speaking, the Bible sees only the inner man (including his thoughts, intentions, desires, emotions, and will) and the outer man (that part of man that is visible to you and me, including his deeds—his words and actions). Only God can see the inner person. Man looks on the outward, "for God sees not as man sees, for man looks at the outward appearance, but the LORD looks at the heart" (1 Samuel 16:7).

As you anticipate change in your eating patterns, keep in mind that your thoughts and your emotions are very closely intertwined. Like the many branches of a vine growing up a wall, it's very difficult to tell where one branch starts and the other ends. How much of what you think can be attributed to your emotions? How much of how you feel can be attributed to your thoughts? It's almost impossible to tell. Then, we add to this mix the way that your physiological state influences and is influenced by both your thoughts and emotions, and we have what appears to be one confused mess.

Here are some examples of how all this works:

1. Your emotions are strongly influenced by your thoughts. You think, *It's not fair for my boss to pass me over for a promotion!* How do your emotions respond? Depending

on your heart, you might respond by getting angry: "I'll show him! I'll make him sorry!"; getting depressed: "I'm just going to quit trying! No one appreciates my work anyway!"; or fear: "Maybe this means that I won't be able to work here much longer. Then what will I do?" Do you see how your *thought* created your *emotional response?*

2. Your thoughts are, in turn, strongly influenced by your emotions. Let's say you feel blue, down, depressed. You begin to think that nothing will ever change. You think that things are worse than they really are. Your thoughts and emotions influence your behavior. You tell your friend that you're sure that nothing will ever change in your situation and you begin to make plans to withdraw completely from that situation. In this case, your *emotions* are affecting your *thoughts.*

3. Your emotions are strongly influenced by your bodily state. If you haven't gotten sufficient sleep, or if you are starving yourself or consistently overeating, your emotions will be affected. You'll feel depressed or fearful or angry. In this instance, your *physical health* affects your *thoughts* and *emotions.*

4. Your *emotions* and *thoughts* can also affect your *physical health.* Everyone knows that if you worry all the time you're liable to get an ulcer. Indeed, the state of the emotions and thoughts can mean the difference between health and sickness for some people.[1]

For clarity's sake, I've illustrated each of these principles below:

1. Thoughts ➡ Emotions

"It's not fair!" ➡ Feelings of anger, depression, fear

2. Emotions ➡ Thoughts

Feeling depressed ➡ "Nothing will ever change"

3. Thoughts & Emotions ➡ Physical Health

"It's not fair!" Feeling angry ➡ Ulcers

4. Physical Health ➡ Thoughts & Emotions
Poor health ➡ "My life is awful"; feeling depressed

In addition to all of this, your *behavior* springs directly out of both your thoughts (which include your desires) and your emotions, so as you are striving to learn godly eating habits, you'll need to think seriously about how your *thoughts* and *emotions* will affect your *eating actions*.

Let's examine how your eating behavior is influenced:

Thoughts ➡ Emotions
"It's not fair!" Feelings of anger, depression, fear
"I'm going to make myself feel better by eating,"
"I'm going to punish them by starving."

Emotions ➡ Thoughts
Feeling depressed ➡ "Nothing will ever change."
"I feel so blue, I deserve to eat something sweet."

Thoughts & Emotions ➡ Physical Health
"It's not fair!" Feeling angry or fearful ➡ high blood pressure, ulcers
"I'm angry so I'm going to overeat, starve, or binge/purge,"
(which creates many health problems).

Physical Health ➡ Thoughts & Emotions
Poor health (for whatever reason) ➡ Thought: "My life is awful."
Feeling depressed; health problems from obesity; bingeing and
purging, and starvation create many sinful thoughts and emotions
including escalating depression, fear, and anger.

As you can see, every part of your inner and outer person is interrelated. And because it's almost impossible to control your raw emotions (such as trying to feel happy or feel love or feel joy), you'll need to learn to get at your emotions through the "back door" of your thoughts and behaviors. I know you're probably wondering how this is done, but for now suffice it to say that the Bible commands us to discipline our thoughts, and it's to this task that we now turn. I'm confident that as we move along, all of this will become very clear. Let's begin by looking at step three in our change process:

*Step Three: Seek diligently to change your
mind and become conformed to
God's thinking, especially in the
area of your eating habits.*

How Should We Think?

God has given some pretty explicit commands regarding our thinking. In fact, in Philippians 4:8, Paul outlines exactly how we are to govern our thoughts. And with good reason—we've just seen how powerful an effect our thoughts can have on our emotions and our actions. Let's look at this passage:

> Finally, brethren, whatever is true, whatever is honorable, whatever is right, whatever is pure, whatever is lovely, whatever is of good repute, if there is any excellence and if anything worthy of praise, *let your mind dwell on these things* (emphasis added).

Paul makes it clear what kinds of thoughts we are to have. We are commanded to "let [our] mind dwell on these things." This isn't a suggestion; it's a command. The word "dwell" here means to make these things the subject of our thoughtful consideration, to carefully reflect on them.

What kinds of thoughts are we to think on? Each one of the adjectives that Paul used is given in the chart on page 141, along with a question that you can use to test how your thoughts fit into the Lord's categories. Whenever you find yourself thinking a certain thought, particularly about your eating habits, you should ask yourself, "Is this thought true, honorable, right, pure, lovely, of good repute, morally excellent, and praiseworthy?"

Let me give you an example of how this might work. Suppose that I've had a hard day at work and I can't wait to get home and have something to eat. As I'm driving home,

WORD	DEFINITION	ASK YOURSELF: *Is this thought . . .*
true	factual	. . . true to the facts, or am I exaggerating or ignoring them? Is it true to the facts that I know about God? His Word? His work? His purpose for me?
honorable	esteemed	. . . something that is beneath me as a daughter of the King? Does it keep my Father's kingship in sight?
right	righteous	. . . reflective of the righteousness that Christ has purchased for me? Or is it part of the way that I thought before I knew His love?
pure	clean	. . . something that I would be ashamed about if others knew I was entertaining it? Does it live up to God's standards of purity and holiness?
lovely	winsome	. . . something that would draw others to Christ? Is it sweet or bitter, beautiful or ugly?
good repute	attractive	. . . a faith-filled assessment of the situation, or does it send my heart trembling in fear away from the Lord?
moral excellence	virtue	. . . overflowing with the excellencies of Christ? Does it acknowledge His great love, mercy, grace, and holiness?
praiseworthy	admirable	. . . something that would cause others to praise God if they heard it? Does it cause my heart to be filled with thanks and worship?

I spend time daydreaming about eating some food and vegging out in front of the television. Traffic is horrible, and by the time I'm close to home, I'm wasted. I decide it's easier to stop at a fast-food restaurant to pick up the family dinner. After I get home and serve up the food, I sit down in front of the television, feeling anxious and irritated, being cranky with my family and filled with ingratitude. "Mom's in one of her moods," the kids whisper. Then, when I discover that my appetite still isn't satisfied, I head for the refrigerator, where I eat every sweet thing in sight. Get the picture?

How did this happen? Where did it start? With the thoughts that I entertained at my desk at work. I'm learning that when I find myself fantasizing in that way, I need to run my thoughts through God's grid of righteous thinking: Is it true that eating and vegging out in front of the television will give me peace and joy? As a daughter of the King of the universe, wouldn't my time be better spent filling my mind with thoughts of His greatness? After all, there's no sense in thinking about food at a time when it's not necessary to do so. Isn't God more precious to me than food? Would I be ashamed if Jesus, the Heart-Knower, was standing right in front of me? Do these thoughts about turning my responsibilities off and the television and my appetites on draw others to Christ? Do they reflect His awesome magnificence? If my co-worker could see into my heart, would she be filled with praise in response to God's greatness, or puzzlement over the way I'm acting?

I know that asking ourselves these questions is a lot of work, but this is what we need to begin practicing if we want to control our thoughts. Again, it's important to learn to control our thoughts because they give birth to our feelings and our actions. That's why we must learn, through diligent practice, to control our thinking. If we spend our day thinking about what we're going to have for dinner, or if we think over and over again about how we think we look fat, we're going to sin either by throwing up, starving ourselves, or giving up in despair and eating everything in sight. It's just a fact that our thoughts, if we entertain them long enough, will turn into action. Frequently we wonder why we acted in a certain way. It is because—whether we're aware of it or not—our thoughts have given birth.

Habitual Thinking

Some of our thoughts are so habitual that we're not always aware that we are thinking them. It's these thoughts that can be among the most difficult to change. You can get at them, though, in one of two ways. The first way is to, by the power of the Holy Spirit, ask God to make you aware of your sinful thoughts. You can do this by keeping a copy of the godly thinking chart on page 141 (it's also in Appendix F) on your desk, your bathroom mirror, or wherever you work. Glance at it from time to time, especially if you have a few free moments to run your thoughts through the grid and see how your thoughts are doing.

The other way to discover your sinful thinking patterns is to work backwards. That is, after you discover you're eating in a sinful way, go back and see what thoughts led to that behavior. Ask the Lord to show you where the seeds of this thinking originated—He will gladly show you, for He desires your best. Realize that as you do this you won't have instant success, but if you don't give up, you'll grow in your ability to recognize your sinful thinking habits. You'll be able to catch wrong thoughts more quickly, which will help you to change the way that you think. This, in turn, will result in more godly eating patterns.

Putting Off and Putting On

How can we free ourselves of sinful thoughts that lead to sinful actions and encourage ourselves to dwell on godly thoughts that lead to godly actions? One way is to identify our sinful thoughts and replace them with godly thoughts. Let's look again at my trip home from the office and see how I could have changed my thinking to prevent sinning.

I'm sitting at my desk at work, and I'm feeling frustrated, anxious, angry, or depressed. Instantly, my thoughts wander to pleasing myself through food. Instead of allowing myself to continue down this path, I stop myself and ask God to help me to put off this way of thinking. I confess to Him that my thoughts were sinful (because they weren't filled with faith or thanksgiving), and thank Him for reminding me about it. I seek to think in new, more godly ways. For instance, I might think, *Things aren't really so bad. I'm thankful that I have a job, and since I know that God put me here, I'm going to concentrate on getting these problems solved instead of feeling sorry for myself. I'm thankful that God has redeemed me—I'm not just some number on a timecard to Him—no, I'm His chosen daughter. I'm thankful that He's put me in this difficult job because He's using it as His means to change me into His image. My attitude can easily influence others and I want to do whatever will give them reason to see God's goodness and greatness. And on the way home in the car, instead of listening to the jazz station and zoning out, I'm going to put on one of my praise tapes and worship Him.*

By redirecting my thoughts, I arrive at an entirely different outcome! And the end result is a happier me, a happier family, a godly influence on those around me, and a God who is glorified. All because I chose to send my thoughts along a different path—a better path! You can do the same in your own life. Ultimately, it comes down to right choices about how you think. Now don't get me wrong—this isn't going to be easy, and you'll certainly have times when you discover yourself back in the old ruts again. But don't be discouraged; God is on your side. This is the process that Paul wrote about in 2 Corinthians 10:5: "We are destroying speculations and every lofty thing raised up against the knowledge of God, and we are taking every thought captive to the obedience of Christ." You need to bring all of your thoughts into submission to Christ's lordship. You can refocus your thoughts, just as the psalmist did: "When my anxious thoughts multiply within me, Thy consolations [comforts] delight my soul" (Psalm 94:19). The psalmist's thoughts reflected anxiety and fear—then he remembered

God's goodness, and the Holy Spirit, the Comforter, delighted his soul.

Treasuring God's Word

Another way you can exchange your sinful thoughts for godly ones is to steep your mind in the Word of God. Job recognized the principle of so meditating on the Word of God that it became what sustained him. He said, "I have not departed from the command of His lips; I have treasured the words of His mouth more than my necessary food" (Job 23:12). Look at that—he esteemed God's Word as more important to him than food! Isn't that incredible? It was because of this love for God's Word that Job was able to make the choices that enabled him to live righteously.

Do you treasure God's Word? Do you look forward to the time of day when you can read it? Do you memorize it? Memorization is one of the keys to meditating on Scripture. We can't walk around with our Bibles open in front of us all day, but we can muse on the Word that's hidden in our heart. We can't hide it in our heart, however, if we don't memorize it. May I suggest that you start memorizing the verses that accompany each of the D-I-S-C-I-P-L-I-N-E-D Eating questions? They are written out in Appendix B. Why not copy them onto index cards so you can carry them with you all the time? Even if you are terrible at memorization, God will help you in this because He longs for you to nourish yourself on His Word. Just start with the first verse, Romans 14:23. Give yourself one week to memorize it. Don't move on to the next verse until you can say this one aloud. Start with the first phrase: "He who doubts is condemned if he eats . . ." and then move on from there, day by day. You'll be surprised at how much you can memorize if you really put your mind to it. Once you finish with the first verse, begin working on the second one without neglecting the first. At the end of 12 weeks you'll have these

12 verses memorized. That will greatly enhance your ability to judge whether your eating is sinful or not.

When it comes to changing eating habits, one of the greatest lessons you'll ever learn is to stop trying to feed your desires with food and to begin to feed your hunger with the Word. That's why Jesus answered Satan in this way when He was tempted: "Man shall not live on bread alone, but on every word that proceeds out of the mouth of God" (Matthew 4:4). Your growth in grace is very dependent upon your consuming God's Word. If you aren't used to reading it every day, just begin with one chapter per day—the Gospel of John would be a good place to start. Record your reading on your daily diary and, before you know it, you will have developed a habit of reading the Bible every day.

Jeremiah said, "Thy words were found and I ate them, and Thy words became for me a joy and the delight of my heart; for I have been called by Thy name, O LORD God of hosts" (Jeremiah 15:16). You'll be able to make that same statement soon. All you need to do is to begin today!

Changing Your Mind

Rebecca, a friend who works for a missionary organization, realized the importance of these lessons. She wrote, "Wrong thinking is what usually triggers wrong eating. As I completed your Bible studies on eating, I began to see how fear, anxiety, and stress were often what triggered my desire to eat incorrectly. Food can be an idol when it replaces God. My comfort needed to be from Him. I needed to practice trusting Him when things got stressful. I needed to let Christ be my reward. This way of thinking wasn't entirely new to me . . . what was different was that I had to squarely face the fact that my eating problem was the result of a choice of mine—refusing to make Christ first in my life, and failing to let Him control my thoughts and actions. I had to be reminded again, after being saved for 24 years, to whom I belong."

It is often said, "It's a woman's prerogative to change her mind." You could rephrase that, "It's a *Christian's* privilege to change her mind." Yes, God *can* help you change your thinking, just as He helped me, and Rebecca, and hundreds of others. He does this by the power of His Holy Spirit as you wait on Him. Even if your thinking is as undisciplined as your eating, and it may well be, He is a great God and He can change even you. Take time now to ask the Lord to help you grow in wisdom in this area. Think about His love, His mercy, His great grace. He certainly is worthy of all our praise!

10

PRACTICE, PRACTICE, PRACTICE

"You shall keep My statutes and practice *them;*
I am the LORD who sanctifies [changes] you."

—LEVITICUS 20:8

*D*uring our second 12-week session together, Kathy was feeling discouraged. She had begun well, but now, at the 18-week mark, she felt like she was walking through a muddy, dark valley with a great burden on her back. "How long am I going to have to work on this problem?" Kathy asked. "It seems as though this is taking forever. It's just so embarrassing and frustrating to have to be focused on this issue all the time. This is the second time I've gone through this program and I'm still learning and struggling. Honestly, I'm really bored with it and I wish that I could move on to something else." The rest of the women in the class all nodded in agreement. Here we were, in the middle of our second session together, and we had all bottomed out.

I know the frustration and impatience that comes with having to struggle over a long period of time with the same

149

behavior. I have been grappling with my sinful eating habits for more than ten years. Please don't misunderstand me. At the beginning of this battle, it wasn't that I didn't know how to go on a diet and lose weight. I had been doing that on and off for my whole life . . . although when I first began to look for God's answer I was about 50 pounds overweight. It was that I was teaching in a Christian school telling my junior high students about God's power to overcome sin, and yet I was completely enslaved to my next meal. I knew that I didn't need to go looking for some new diet. I had already done that more times than I could remember. I had longed to experience God's life-changing power as evidenced in the Bible and in other areas in my life. I began to search for some answer, some key to this weakness. Perhaps I needed to pray in a certain way, or have someone with a lot of faith pray for me. Certainly God could help me with this problem, couldn't He?

I remember the night when I took my first step on the journey that has brought me here to you. I had been reading in 2 Peter, and there right before my eyes was the truth I had been searching for. Let me share this powerful verse with you: "His divine power has granted to us *everything* pertaining to life and godliness, through the true knowledge of Him who called us by His own glory and excellence" (2 Peter 1:3, emphasis added). God, by His power, had already given me *everything* that I needed to grow in life and godliness! This thought struck me like a thunderbolt! I didn't need to search around any longer. I didn't need to keep hoping for some new breakthrough in my faith. The answers were all there, with Him, in the power of His Spirit and His Word.

But that was just the beginning. For more than ten years now I've been learning and growing in my understanding of the great resources God has provided to make change possible in my life. And it's taken me years to see the transformation that I have longed for. Yet still there are times when I find myself slipping into my old ways of thinking and acting. These times have become much fewer, thank God, and I know that change really is possible. But because eating is so much a part of life, and because eating patterns are so habitual, changing them has had to become one of the main endeavors of my life. I've had to learn to practice godliness on a day-in and day-out basis, year after year—and thank God, He's been faithful to honor my desire to glorify Him with victory in my life. I know that He can do the same thing for you. This journey won't be over in six weeks, or even in six months. No, the journey toward godliness takes a lifetime . . . but don't despair, He will be with you all the way, giving you the encouragement to carry on.

A Slow, Steady Growth

In our modern, microwave, zap-it-for-ten-seconds culture, we have become extremely impatient. We believe so strongly in our own ability to find quick and easy answers that we get frustrated when things take time. The kinds of changes that God desires to make in us will take time—there's no denying that. If you're feeling anxious to get this over with and wondering if there is something wrong with you because you aren't getting it, then this chapter is especially for you.

You may be wondering, *Isn't God powerful enough to change me immediately?* Yes, God can (and sometimes does) bring about instantaneous changes in His children's lives. I know that there are people who are instantly delivered from drug addiction, for instance, and although I rejoice in this, I don't believe that's typical. Indeed, the New Testament affirms that the most common method for sanctification (change) is a process that has to be *practiced* as you struggle against sin. This struggle is used by God to increase your hatred of your sin and your love for Him; it causes you to be humble and continue to rely on Him; it "trains your hands for war." [1] God has many uses for abiding sin, [2] and we must resist the discouragement that would tempt us to seek after a different method (something quicker, easier!) than His own.

Let's review our four steps again. Remember that I said they would seem overly simplistic and also too difficult? By now we can see why: With God's help, it's possible for change to happen. Yet we need to cooperate with Him, which means denying daily the fleshly desires that can hinder our progress toward change. In addition, we've seen that true change requires internal adjustments in our minds and attitudes—it's not just a matter of food intake and exercise.

While all this requires more work than we may have originally anticipated, I can assure you of one thing: This is the best kind of change we can pursue because every step of the way we're relying on God's methods for bringing about the desired results. So let's continue to hang in there together, because the rewards of following God's ways are well worthwhile!

Relying upon the Holy Spirit you must:

1. *Become convinced that your present method of eating is sinful and cease from it;*

2. *Become convinced that God's methods for disciplined eating are right and begin practicing them;*

3. *Seek diligently to change your mind and become conformed to God's thinking, especially in the area of your eating habits; and*

4. *Continue to practice these new thoughts and behaviors, even when the struggle gets hard.*

We're now ready to look at step four, which is a reminder to us that we need to diligently practice the first three steps until they become second nature. Soon you won't have to look at the D-I-S-C-I-P-L-I-N-E-D Eating questions every day. In any given food situation, you'll know immediately if you're about to cross over the line.

Practicing Godliness

Growth in godliness is not easy. It is something that we must practice or work at. A righteous lifestyle involves labor. Sometimes I've encountered an attitude in myself that basically says, "If God wants me to be godly, He knows where I live. He can zap me anytime He wants." Such an attitude reflects a lack of seriousness about my spiritual growth. It also plays into my personal laziness and desire to cut corners.

The Bible is filled with admonitions to practice godliness, including this one in 1 Timothy 4:7: "Have nothing to do with godless myths and old wives' tales; rather, train yourself to be godly" (NIV). If you want something more than a diet that will merely help you to lose (or gain) 20 pounds without really looking at the heart-change that you need, then you will to have to work at it just as I have.

The verb "train" in 1 Timothy 4:7 means "exercise" or "discipline." The term that was used in the Greek text actually means "to train naked" (better not take that literally!). I know that this sounds peculiar and I don't mean that you should go to the gym without any attire. No, the point that Paul is making here is that you must *strip away everything that might hinder your growth in godliness*. Impatience, laziness, or unbelief will hinder your training in the same way that long, flowing robes would trip a runner. When I go to the gym or on a long walk I purposely pick out clothing that won't bind or hinder my movements in any way. I don't want to be distracted from my exercise by having to mess with my clothes. Likewise, Paul is saying that you should seek to develop a lifestyle of thinking and acting that won't trip you up or distract you from your goal. Impatience with the race is a particularly typical and ensnaring robe. Throw it off today. Ask yourself, "Why am I being so impatient? Is it pride, or laziness, or . . . ?" When you think about it, there's no reason to be impatient. *We don't have anything else in our life that's more important than allowing God to change us, do we?*

There are many, many verses in the Bible that talk about practicing godliness. Let's look at just a few of them:

- "You shall keep My statutes and *practice them*; I am the LORD who sanctifies [changes] you" (Leviticus 20:8).

- "Ezra had set his heart to study the law of the LORD, *and to practice it* . . ." (Ezra 7:10).

- "How blessed are those who keep justice, who *practice righteousness at all times!*" (Psalm 106:3).

- "The things you have learned and received and heard and seen in me, *practice these things*; and the God of peace shall be with you" (Philippians 4:9).

It is not part of anyone's nature to respond to life in godly ways. Julie, a friend who battled bulimia, wondered why it was so hard for her to grow in godliness. She desired to please God and yet, on Sunday morning (after an agonizing struggle with her sinful habits all week), she would frequently look around the congregation and wonder why it seemed that all the other women were so holy, so godly. She saw their smiling faces, their perfect bodies, and she was filled with despair and discouragement. She thought that there must be something intrinsically different or wrong with her. Perhaps it was because of her upbringing. Maybe she just wasn't cut out to be a godly woman. *Why can't I be like other women?* she wondered.

Julie grew in godliness when she realized that everyone struggles with sin—not just her. And yet it does seem as though there are certain people who are godly. I'm sure that you have known some. What makes them different? Were they born with a propensity to be more godly? I don't think that anyone is born with an advantage when it comes to godliness. We have all inherited a sinful nature from our forefathers.[3] In addition, our own hearts and our environment have taught us to sin. Now, I'm not saying that a Christian upbringing is useless for helping deal with life's battles. It's just that when it comes to real change—to practicing godliness over the long haul—no one has any real advantage over anyone else.

So, then, why are some people more godly than others? I believe it is because they *practice* the truth that they have received. What was Paul's advice to the Philippian believers? In essence, he said, "Whatever you've seen me do— whatever I've taught you and you have believed, you must *practice* those things." You see, it's not enough to just hear the truth. The apostle James wrote that merely hearing the truth without practicing it is self-deceptive:

> Prove yourselves doers of the word, and not merely hearers who delude themselves. For if anyone is a hearer of the word and not a doer, he is like a man who looks at his natural face in a mirror; for once he has looked at himself and gone away, he has immediately forgotten what kind of person he was. But one who looks intently at the perfect law, the law of liberty, and abides by it, not having become a forgetful hearer but an effectual doer, this man shall be blessed in what he does (James 1:22-25).

James says that hearing the truth and then walking away from it is like a man looking at his face in the mirror, discovering that it is dirty, and then walking away without doing anything about it. The man could stand at the mirror and take care of the problem by washing his face, but instead, he ignores the problem and walks away. He chooses not to respond. Or, perhaps he responds by splashing a little water on his face for a moment or two, and then when he discovers that his face will need a real scrubbing, he decides that it really isn't that important after all and walks away. What's terrifying about this kind of behavior is that after a while, the man will be so used to seeing his face dirty that he won't even notice anything is amiss. He will think he's just fine and that a dirty face is normal. He won't understand why everyone else makes such a fuss about washing up.

So it isn't enough for us to splash water on our face once or twice. Finding out what the Bible teaches about D-I-S-C-I-P-L-I-N-E-D Eating isn't the end of the process. No, our habits need a radical change, and this change isn't accomplished by one or two days, weeks, or even months of sporadic effort. We must commit to practice, practice, practice. And then, when we think we've got it, we must practice some more.

Habitual Godliness

Think again about what we've learned about habits. We've learned that the capacity to form habits is a wonderful blessing from God. Without it, our days would be filled with frustration and discouragement. Also, we have the capacity to form godly habits in just the same ways that we formed our present ungodly ones. The strength and ease of our present habits ought to encourage us that we—all of us—can form godly habits.

I've recommended that you begin to establish some new habits. I know that at first these new patterns will seem difficult, uncomfortable, or strange. For example, shortly before writing this chapter, our family moved into a new house. Everything that was habitual and second nature to me about the old house is now gone. In the new house, I don't know which way the cabinets open. I have to think about where the water heater is. I don't know the quickest way to get from the family room to the front yard—should I go through the garage or out the front door? I'm not used to the sprinklers coming on in the morning, and I still wake up wondering what that noise is. I'm still testing to see which light switches turn on which lights. Because of all the changes I'm having to make, the amount of time and extra effort that I must expend just to do my everyday tasks is tremendous. In fact, I've been I'm reading the manual on how to operate the dishwasher!

I can imagine that as you are moving into new ways of thinking and acting with your eating you are just as uncomfortable as I found myself to be in my new house (even though the new home is a real blessing to me). I want to encourage you to not give up. Yes, it'll take extra time and effort to ask yourself the **D-I-S-C-I-P-L-I-N-E-D** Eating questions and to record everything I've asked you to record. I know that you feel like you just don't have the time. But keep this in mind: After a while, you'll begin to think this way automatically—and even though you'll have to keep practicing the disciplines, it will become easier to do so in time. Don't despair—remember the power of the Holy Spirit!

Because step four has to do with the practice of our disciplines, let's see how life looks when we apply what we're learning.

Putting It All into Practice

The D-I-S-C-I-P-L-I-N-E-D *Eating Questions*

You'll want to take the **D-I-S-C-I-P-L-I-N-E-D** Eating questions, copy them, and put them up on your refrigerator and any place you normally eat (your car? your office?). You'll find an abbreviated version of these questions in Appendix A. As for the verses that go along with the questions, you'll want to copy them onto index cards and begin to memorize them (spiral-bound note cards are very handy for that). Keep the cards in your purse or pocket, and when you're stuck in line at the grocery store or waiting for little Johnny to be done with the dentist, whip them out and work on memorizing both the questions (or at least the first word of the acrostic) and the verses that accompany them.

The Daily Diary

Recording Food Choices

Have you started using the daily diary? There's no better time to start than today! You have permission to make copies of the diary pages for your own personal use. If you want to enlarge the diary for easier use, please feel free to do so. Remember that it's important to be very specific about the types and amounts of food that you eat—and since we tend to forget what we've eaten, it's best to write it down as soon as you eat it. I've created a space for each of the major food groups.[4] Appendix D has a completed daily diary so you can see how the diary is to be used. You can put fats and sweets in the "Other" category. Next to your food choice, indicate whether you violated any of the D-I-S-C-I-P-L-I-N-E-D Eating questions. You can do so by looking at the questions and then looking at what you ate. Next to a wrong food choice, you can simply write the first letter of the corresponding word, for instance, "D" for "Doubt" or "I" for "Idolatry." Because some letters repeat themselves, you may want to think of a way of distinguishing them. For instance, you could write "Do" for "Doubt" and "Dt" for "Distract."

Whatever way you decide to designate each word is fine, just as long as you stick with it so that you're establishing habits and so that, by the end of the week, you'll be able to look over your diary and circle the letters that appear three or more times. This will help you get to know your problem areas. For example, if you find that "L" for "Life" appears almost every day, then you need to ask God to help you concentrate on viewing your body as His temple. Perhaps you'll need to review the part of the book that deals with this truth (chapter 4—We Are God's Temple) and ask Him to help you in the ways outlined in that chapter.

No matter what your problem areas on the daily diary, you can ask the Holy Spirit to make you aware of the desires and situations that most tempt you and to help you change your thinking.

There is absolutely no way for you to be aware of your eating habits, discover your particular weaknesses, and grow past them if you aren't reflecting on them daily. I know that this seems like a lot to ask, but if you keep your daily diary with you and then reflect on it at night before you go to sleep, you'll be able to see your progress and be encouraged. You'll be able to rejoice in the victory that God brings and you'll find yourself very motivated to say no to bad food choices.

If at the end of the day you discover that you've sinned in your eating in some way, take time *right then* to ask God to forgive you and to help you to avoid this sin. Ask Him to keep you from this temptation and to make you aware when you are in danger. Ask Him to show you the desires of your heart that caused this temptation to seem appealing.

Drinking Water

On the daily diary there is also a place for you to indicate your water intake. Drinking water during the day is extremely important for a number of reasons. First, water is beneficial to the proper functioning of your body. Your body needs water to accomplish many of its tasks, so you are protecting and nourishing God's temple when you learn to drink it regularly. Most of us drink so little water that our body is always in a state of dehydration. If your body is dehydrated, you will retain water and feel bloated and uncomfortable. Second, water assists in the metabolizing of fat, which will also help you to be more healthy. Third, if you are drinking a lot of water, you are less likely to confuse hunger and thirst. Hunger/thirst confusion is very common among overeaters, and drinking plenty of water will train your palate to distinguish between the two. Fourth, if you have difficulty staying regular, particularly when you're controlling your eating, water will be of great benefit to you.

I've placed three little boxes in the water category and I recommend that you drink approximately 20 ounces of water three times a day—during the morning, noon, and evening. If you find that you're up all night running to the restroom, then you might want to stop drinking your water by 6:00 P.M. or so. Whether you do this exactly or not is your decision; it's just that drinking about eight 8-ounce glasses of water is generally recommended by health professionals. I myself try to keep one of those 32-ounce bottles on my desk and sip from it during the day. At first this will seem like a lot of water (and you'll be running to the restroom frequently), but you'll get used to it, and then, if you don't have your water, you'll feel very thirsty. That's good!

Calorie or Fat Total

In the daily diary is a "Cal/Fat Total" box for you to use if you choose to count calories or fat grams or if you are on an eating program that encourages this. You can keep track of your expenditures during the day and then total them in this category.

Please remember that just because you've eaten only 1,200 calories and had less than 50 grams of fat in a day, doesn't mean that your eating is pleasing to the Lord. On the other hand, if you find that you usually over- or undereat, you might want to keep track of these totals until you establish more controlled eating habits. Diets like the ones that I have recommended are fine but should be approached only as a guideline for your eating. Just because the diet allows certain foods doesn't mean that it is okay for you to indulge in them. It would be wonderful if, after really learning how to eat in a truly godly fashion, you wouldn't need to think about diets any longer. But diets can provide beneficial outer control that will help guide you in your endeavor to make your eating habits pleasing to God. Choose any eating plan that you like—as long as it is nutritionally sound, doesn't promise instant weight loss, and doesn't violate any of the D-I-S-C-I-P-L-I-N-E-D Eating questions.

Recording Spiritual Disciplines

Prayer Time

Record the time of day that you pray, such as 7:00 A.M. each day. I encourage you to make an effort to pray at the same time every day so that prayer becomes a habit.

As for what to pray about, you may find the old acrostic A-C-T-S very helpful. Start with "A" for "Adoration." Take time to thank God for who He is, to praise Him, and rejoice in His greatness. Speak to Him about His exceedingly magnificent character. "Men shall speak of the power of Thine awesome acts; and I will tell of Thy greatness" (Psalm 145:6). As you do this you will glorify Him and build up your own faith.

"C" stands for "Confession." Take time to reflect on the ways that your thoughts, words, or deeds have failed to meet His standard of holiness and love. Ask Him for His forgiveness. He is faithful to forgive all your sin, no matter if you've asked a hundred times before, because He's so merciful. He has promised, "If we confess our sins, He is faithful and righteous to forgive us our sins and to cleanse us from all unrighteousness" (1 John 1:9). Yes, that applies even to you, even to your eating.

"T" stands for "Thanksgiving." I know that if I don't take time every day to thank God for what He's done for me, pretty soon I get discontented and covetous. The best antidote to a grumbling, unbelieving heart is to give thanks daily. Why not make a list of the things that you are thankful for and then recite them at your prayer time? You'll find that your heart is more inclined to overflow with gratitude when you just stop and consider what God has done for you. Even if you feel like you are at the very bottom of the lowest pit, you can always thank God that, at least right now, you can take a breath. That's a gift from Him, and your step toward cultivating a thankful heart will lift you up from the doldrums of discontent and unbelief.

There are so many wonderful verses on thanksgiving! Let me give you three from the Psalms:

> Thou hast turned for me my mourning into dancing; Thou hast loosed my sackcloth and girded me with gladness; that my soul may sing praise to Thee, and not be silent. O LORD my God, I will give thanks to Thee forever (Psalm 30:11-12).

> I will give thanks to Thee, O Lord my God, with all my heart, and will glorify Thy name forever. For Thy lovingkindness toward me is great, and Thou hast delivered my soul from the depths of Sheol (Psalm 86:12-13).

> It is good to give thanks to the LORD, and to sing praises to Thy name, O Most High; to declare Thy lovingkindness in the morning, and Thy faithfulness by night (Psalm 92:12).

Developing a genuinely thankful heart is one of the best defenses against sin because sin is always a statement that you believe God hasn't provided for your needs.

Finally, "S" stands for "Supplication." It is only after you've adored, confessed, and thanked God that your heart is ready to supplicate. It's only after you've delighted yourself in Him that He rejoices to give you the desires of your heart.[5] I'm not saying it's wrong to ask God to meet your needs; in fact, He wants you to do so. It's just that if you run into His presence like a petulant little child, demanding your own way, you'll find a shallowness and weakness in your prayers. If you study the pattern presented in the

Lord's Prayer (Matthew 6:9-13), you'll find that praying about your own needs comes just about last on the list. This is good for us because it's easy to lose sight of the fact that life is not really about us and our kingdom, but about God and His kingdom.

If you have not set a regular time yet for prayer, I trust you'll begin to practice this discipline today. If you feel you don't have enough time to pray, remember that God will help you make time, since it's His desire for you to seek Him. If you have to, combine your prayer time with something else, like exercise, or even driving to work. However, the ideal would be to focus your complete attention on prayer, if you can. If that means locking yourself in the bathroom for 15 minutes of solitude once a day, then do it. Susanna Wesley, who had more children and responsibilities than most of us, used to pull her apron up over her head and pray. If you set up a regular time of solitude for prayer, your children will learn not to disturb you, and they will also learn that you believe that prayer is important.

While we're on the subject of prayer, let me also encourage you to get into the habit of thanking God for your food before you eat it. Remember that 1 Timothy 4:4 tells us that our food is set apart for our use by grateful prayer, so train yourself to stop before you put anything in your mouth and let your thanks be known to the Lord.

Bible Reading

Under the category "Bible Chpts," indicate which chapters you read that day. For instance, you could write, "Jn 1 & 2" for Monday, "Jn 3 & 4" for Tuesday, and so on. As we discovered earlier, our Bible reading is as important as our meals. We're called to hide God's Word in our heart, feast on His Words, and to not live by bread alone but by every word that proceeds from His mouth. It's only as you saturate your mind with the Bible that you will make progress in changing your thinking. To fight my propensity to fly through my reading without taking the time to understand or think about it, I read aloud. My hope is that if I *hear* the text as well as read it, I'll be more likely to comprehend and digest it.

You'll find it helpful to have a Bible that you can understand and feel comfortable writing in. I personally use the New American Standard Bible, but you can use the King James (original or new) or the New International Version, if you prefer.[6] If you find a verse that is particularly meaningful to you, go ahead and underline it or make a note next to it in the margin. In time, your Bible will become filled with notes that indicate your growth in the understanding of His wonderful truth.

Recording Physical Disciplines

Most of us live very sedentary lives and need exercise to stay in good health. By making exercise a part of your daily or weekly routine, you'll reap great benefits. Exercising regularly will give you more energy, help you to sleep better at night, and help to relieve your stress. If you exercise aerobically, your brain will release endorphins into your bloodstream, which will give you a sense of well-being. And if you are overweight, exercise is an important key to weight loss.

As with any new regimen, you must begin your exercise program prudently. It's not necessary for you to become a member at a gym. You can keep it as simple as walking regularly in the evening. If you don't live in a neighborhood where it's safe to walk, consider going to the local mall. We have mall-walkers at one of our larger local malls. These are mostly seniors who show up before the stores open in the morning and walk for half an hour or so. In most communities there are also walking clubs or groups. Why not get a friend to join you? The companionship will help make the time pass more quickly.

If you are more adventurous (and can afford it), you can always join a gym or buy exercise equipment. My own personal experience is that I do much better going to the gym then I do riding an exercise bike in the garage. I'm just more motivated and there are less distractions at the gym. In addition, I can take a step class or a low-impact aerobic class and get a pretty good workout in about an hour.

Generally speaking, you should exercise to the point of increased heart rate and breathing at least 3 times per week and sustain this exercise for at least 20 minutes. Of course, if you haven't exercised in years, don't try to play an active game of tennis right away. A quick stroll will suffice—fast enough to get away from someone who might be following you, and slow enough to not tip them off that you know he or she is there. If you don't have a friend who can join you, then grab a praise tape and headphones, and off you go. Start small, and work up. If you overdo your exercise you could injure yourself so that you can't do anything for months.

This may seem hard to believe if exercise isn't a part of your lifestyle, but there are women who overexercise—particularly those who struggle with bulimia and anorexia. Here are a number of questions you can ask yourself to determine whether you're exercising too much:

- Do you feel guilty if a day goes by when you don't work out?

- Are you depressed if you are unable to exercise?

- Do you feel tired and lethargic, yet still have trouble sleeping?

- Do you have injuries that don't seem to heal?

- Are you reluctant to take time off to heal injuries?

- Are you ignoring aspects of your work, social life, or family life in order to exercise?

- Do you feel compelled to work out even if you are tired?

- Do you increase or decrease your exercise based on your weight or what you have eaten?

- Do you suffer from insomnia, undesired weight loss, fatigue, lethargy, irritability, loss of menstrual periods, multiple chronic injuries, or stress fractures?[7]

If you answered yes to several of the above questions, you are probably exercising too much. You can injure yourself or so tax your body that you end up violating the Sixth Commandment. You must seek to develop self-control, even if that means moderating your exercise so that you aren't answering yes to the questions just stated.

Be sure to record your exercise in the space given on the daily diary. You could write, "Walked 3 miles," or "Step Class—one hour." If you can exercise moderately and consistently, you'll find that your body will respond very quickly.

Although exercise is beneficial, some Christians think that it isn't important. To support their viewpoint, they quote Paul's words that "bodily discipline [exercise] is only of little profit" (1 Timothy 4:8). When Paul wrote these words, however, he was comparing bodily exercise (which offers temporary benefits) to godliness (which profits eternally). In making that comparision he wasn't saying that Christians shouldn't try to keep their bodies as healthy as possible. Rather, he was stating that this kind of training profits for just a short time—while we're here on earth. Keep in mind that Paul lived in a world that didn't have cars, computers, and big comfy sofas with televisions and remote controls for everything. The typical early church member had to walk to get water, had to tend a garden for food, had to keep flocks. No one sat around all day staring at a screen of some sort. To tell those people that they needed to exercise to be healthy was ridiculous. We live in a very different world, however. For most of us, aside from those who labor with their bodies, exercise is something that must be scheduled into our lives.

Victories

Under the "Victories" column, you'll want to jot down one or two words that will help jog your memory at the end of the week. For example, you could write, "No idolatry!" if you made it through a day without making food your god. At the end of the week, when you might be feeling like you haven't made much progress, you'll be able to review the victories column and see that God is indeed changing you—maybe slowly, but surely.

Needed Growth

If you find that you continue to struggle in a certain area—like remembering to pray or read Scripture—you could enter these items in the "Needed Growth" column. Or, at the end of the week, if you notice that "Idolatry" has occurred more than three times and thus you need to work on that area of your eating habits, you could write that down as well.

Personal Growth Sheet

The women from my uncommon vessels class developed a "Personal Growth Sheet" to track their progress and struggles with the D-I-S-C-I-P-L-I-N-E-D Eating principles. If you would like to keep a concise track of your changes, you can do so on Appendix E, page 247. Permission is granted to reproduce this chart.

Finding an Accountability Partner

Let me give you one last suggestion: Since we all do better when we know that someone is watching us and praying for us, I recommend that you find an accountability partner. This could be a family member, a close friend who is working on the same problem as you, or it could be a spiritually mature woman in your church. Let her know that you'd like to show her your daily diary at periodic intervals (weekly or bimonthly) so that you'll be more motivated to fill it out consistently.

Heart-Change Is Possible!

Getting into the habit of using the daily diary will benefit you, just as it has hundreds of others. "I never knew how much food I ate until I began using the diary," is a comment I've heard over and over again. Other women who had never been able to establish a consistent prayer life began to do so with the help of the diary. The consistent recording of the spiritual disciplines helped them to see not only the areas of needed growth, but also their progress. The diary gave them the capacity to review their eating choices and see concrete changes. This "feedback" gave them encouragement and helped motivate them to continue doing better!

I hope that you are encouraged now and believe that *you* can change. The steps that I've outlined are attainable by anyone who knows the Lord and who really desires to change. Remember that you won't be perfect at this—especially not at first. But as you practice, practice, and practice, you'll find that the changes you've longed for will eventually become second nature. Yes, even for you.

11

A WORD SPECIFICALLY
FOR YOU

"Little children, guard yourselves from idols."

—1 JOHN 5:21

*I*n this chapter I'm going to devote time to looking at three destructive eating behaviors:
anorexia, bulimia, and compulsive overeating.
Even if you don't habitually practice any of these behaviors, let me encourage you to read this chapter anyway
because you may find it helpful to know the dynamics that
are involved in them.

For several reasons that I have included in the endnotes
to this chapter,[1] I am not comfortable using the labels
anorexia, *bulimia*, and *compulsive*. For the sake of brevity,
however, I'll just refer you to those notes. Please understand
that when I use these terms, I don't mean that anorexia,
bulimia, or compulsive overeating are diseases in the same
sense that polio is a disease. I believe that they are chosen,
life-dominating behaviors. Since we are responsible for
them, we can have the hope that, as we rely on the power of
the Holy Spirit, we can change.

169

I fully understand that the behaviors involved in binge eating, purging, and self-starvation seem so strong, so involuntary, that it *appears* that they are diseases. We feel like we can't control them. We *feel* drawn to the refrigerator. This feeling is a strong physical sensation. We feel like we have an illness. I do recognize the enslaving power of sinful habits. I know that these life-dominating sins *feel* like sickness. We *feel* so helpless—like we're being attacked from outside. Let me encourage you once again to not look for the answer that seems easy, but instead to press on to find God's truth about your problems.

Everything that I have said so far in this book can be applied to all three categories of destructive eating behaviors. I understand that you will have to take these truths and tailor them to your particular behavior, but I believe that, at heart, each one involves the same issue: an inordinate love for or focus on food, which the Bible calls *gluttony*. There are, of course, differences in how this excessive focus on food is played out. Let's take time to look at some of the unique differences, and then seek a fuller understanding of God's perspective on them.

Defining the Terms

Anorexia Nervosa is habitual, self-induced starvation resulting in extreme weight loss. This weight loss is usually accomplished through rigid dieting, radical exercise routines, and purging, or any combination of these measures.

Bulimia, which literally means "ox-like appetite," is characterized by the consumption of large quantities of food, which is usually followed by some type of purging behavior, such as self-induced vomiting, overuse of laxatives, overexercising, or self-imposed starvation.

Compulsive overeating is the practice of habitually overeating when not hungry, feeling "out of control" around food, eating large amounts of food without really tasting or enjoying it, or habitually eating when emotionally upset or to nurture yourself.

As you can see, the person who practices any of these behaviors is not your general run-of-the-mill dieter who works for a couple of weeks to lose five or ten pounds before her class reunion. No, the person who practices them is completely overcome by them. The pleasure or satisfaction derived from them is extremely short-lived, if present at all, and the enslaving power of these habits is immense. That's why I believe it is appropriate to refer to them as life-dominating practices. Every facet of the anorectic's life—her thoughts, words, actions, and desires—is influenced and controlled by her desire to be thin.

The Physiological Effects

The habitual practice of anorexia (self-starvation) also results in very serious deterioration of the body, including the cessation of menstruation and diminishing thyroid function, resulting in brittle hair and nails, dry skin, cold intolerance, and constipation. With the depletion of fat, the body temperature becomes lower. A delicate, downy hair (lanugo) forms over the skin. Electrolyte imbalance creates irregular heart rhythms, heart failure, and decreased bone density.[2]

The habitual practice of bulimia has many serious physiological effects: the erosion of the esophagus and teeth, increased inability to digest food, involuntary vomiting, bowel irregularity or extreme diarrhea, absence of menstruation, slow or irregular heartbeat, subnormal body temperature, and growth of lanugo. Although the bulimic usually maintains weight within normal ranges, there are frequent fluctuations depending on binges, purges, diets, and fasts.

Habitually overeating, which almost always causes obesity, has many damaging results. Obesity is a known risk factor for diabetes, heart disease, high blood pressure, gallbladder disease, arthritis, breathing problems, and some forms of cancer.[3]

If you practice any of the behaviors described above, it is very important for you to be evaluated and cared for by a physician, even if you aren't presently exhibiting any of these symptons. And if you do have symptoms, please do not neglect to see a doctor—ignoring the physical problems won't make them go away and may, in fact, make them significantly worse. All three of these behaviors can lead to severe medical problems and even death.

I think that it is safe to say that most women who are entrapped by these behaviors never planned to be. I don't believe that anyone plans to be bulimic. In both anorexia and bulimia, perhaps the woman began the behavior as a method to control weight and then found herself feeling that she was unable to stop. For the woman who compulsively overeats, running to food simply became the way that she handled the ups and downs she faced in life.

Although everyone is unique and our personal motives are all very different, I think that it is safe to say that there is a dynamic of idolatry in all life-dominating sins, including gluttony. To help you understand how this dynamic functions, let's read about Marlene, a woman who practiced bulimia. I realize that if you are anorectic or a compulsive overeater you will have to adjust this example for your situation, so after I've thoroughly explained Marlene's behavior, I'll give you more specific guidance.

A Life-Dominating Struggle

I hope that you have a clear enough understanding of idolatry from your reading so far that you understand what I mean when I say that bulimics have adopted "a different god." Remember that an idol is anything that usurps your love for God. If you are bulimic, you must ask yourself, *What do I love, seek after, or worship more than God?* I imagine that this might be a difficult question for you to answer, so let's examine Marlene's struggle with bulimia to see what she loved, sought after, and worshiped.

Marlene was a 24-year-old married Christian mother of two when I first met her. She had practiced habits of bulimia since high school. As I got to know her it became apparent that one of the main goals of her life was to be thinner than her sisters. She had first embraced this thought in junior high and had never really grown past it. *"I must be thinner than my sisters,"* was so strong in her desires that it actually functioned as a god to her, even though she wasn't always fully aware of it. Her obsession dictated the focus of her thoughts and actions. It ruled over her, demanding enslaving obedience. It was a ruthless taskmaster.

The worship of her god, *"I must be thinner than my sisters,"* had a number of different nuances. For instance, her identity and worth as a woman were tied up in what size she wore. Her daily experience of peace and joy was determined by whether she was "good" or "bad" in her eating. Her emotions alternated between anger and frustration because she spent her life in such futility; she felt depressed and fearful that she would never change, and she was filled with self-loathing and self-indulgence. These emotions gave rise to more despair, disgust, and bitterness, leading her to eat everything in sight. Marlene wanted to serve the Lord and after each binge, she would resolve again to live her life for Christ. But she continually found her thoughts focused on the questions, *What do I look like? Am I gaining weight? Am I as good as they are?* As a result, her relationships with her family were affected. Every family gathering was ruined by fear. When Marlene saw her sisters she immediately compared herself with them—had they gained weight? Was she more in control than they? Did they compliment her on her figure? Would they criticize her for being too thin or too fat? Her god perverted every joyful occasion, leeching out the pleasure of family, creating an atmosphere of competition, fear, and ambition in her own heart. Would they eat two helpings of turkey? She would have only one . . . did they notice?

Life-Dominating Demands

As we look at Marlene's struggles, we learn that every god demands worship and service. Marlene's god, *"I must be thinner than my sisters,"* demanded that Marlene constantly think about how she looked, and how her clothing fit—no matter whether she had eaten any sugar the day before. What the scale said to her about her weight determined whether she had peace or anxiety. She worshiped the thought of wearing a size 5; she spent far too much time and money on her appearance. Her treasure and her heart were tied up in her bodily image. Functionally, she believed that if she could just serve her god perfectly enough she would have abundant life—she would know true peace and joy. She was utterly and tragically consumed by her god's demands.

Self-Centered Laws

Marlene's god, *"I must be thinner than my sisters,"* had also created commandments that she had to follow. These laws were: "Thou shalt not eat sugar," "Thou shalt not eat potato chips," "Thou shalt burn off at least 500 calories in exercise every day." She felt more peaceful, more *in control*, when she followed these laws. The problem was that she could never perfectly satisfy her god's demands because idols are never satisfied with your version of perfection. No, idols create laws that multiply exponentially. At one time it had been all right for her to eat some sugar, just as long as it wasn't in chocolate. Eventually, all sugar became unlawful. When Marlene didn't obey these laws, she experienced a greater sense of futility, anger, and desperation. Let me illustrate Marlene's problem this way:

Her god:

"I must be thinner than my sisters"
created

Her god's laws (which had to be perfectly obeyed):

THOU SHALT NOT EAT SUGAR.
THOU SHALT NOT EAT POTATO CHIPS.
THOU SHALT EXERCISE OFF 500 CALORIES PER DAY.

When Marlene "sinned" and violated the laws she had devised in her heart, she would usually respond by feeling angry and, in despair, giving in to her self-indulgence. However, there were some days when she would "regain control" and would respond by rededicating her efforts to be "perfect" for the rest of the day, by exercising more than usual to make up for her mistake, and by promising to be very careful for the rest of the week.

On the days when Marlene gave in to self-indulgence and despair, she would stop on the way home from work and buy food to consume while driving home. Upon arriving home, she would raid the pantry. She would eat everything in sight—very rapidly, very secretly. Then, she would seek to atone for her transgressions by throwing up in the kitchen sink—all this before her husband got home. We could diagram her behavior in this way:

Her god:
"I must be thinner than my sisters"
created

Her god's law (which had to be perfectly obeyed):

THOU SHALT NOT EAT SUGAR.
THOU SHALT NOT EAT POTATO CHIPS.
THOU SHALT EXERCISE OFF 500 CALORIES PER DAY.

Marlene transgresses her god's law (sins)
by eating a cookie, so she . . .

Realizes that she won't attain her goal of
perfection that day, so she . . .

Is worried, angry, and fearful because
she has failed again, so she . . .

Self-indulges (the binge) in a feeble attempt
to demonstrate her disgust, assuage her guilty
conscience, bring pleasure to herself by
throwing off restraint, resulting in . . .

The need for a savior from her "sin" and its results
(stomach discomfort/weight gain), so she . . .

Embraces her "savior," the "purge" (vomiting, laxatives,
overexercising, fasting), and then she . . .

Recommits to renewed measures to maintain her
self-righteousness and please her god: "I'll never
do this again" and "I'll do better tomorrow"
were her mantras, which seemed to work until she
violated her conscience again by breaking a law or
was frustrated by some circumstance in her life,
at which time the cycle would start over again.

Do you see what I mean when I say that these behaviors are life-dominating? Almost every waking moment was tyrannized by thoughts, emotions, and actions—all relating to her false god.

Recognizing Erroneous Thoughts

If in some way I've just described you, please don't despair. Your loving Father in heaven is able to break sin's power and lead you on to victory—to help you become a person whose life and love is solely focused on pleasing Him. I watched Him change Marlene, and I know He can change you, too.

Some of the more typical thoughts that function as idols are listed below. See if any of them ring a bell in your heart.

If you are anorectic or bulimic, then you may be able to relate to some of the following thoughts:

- Perhaps you have believed our culture's lies about appearance: "You have worth only if you are thin." "Fat people are losers." "Only thin people are truly happy." Your god might be *"I must be thin so that I can have worth."*

- Perhaps your mother was overweight and dieting all the time and you just can't stand to think that you'll spend your life like her: "I'll never be out of control like she is." "She's so weak. I'm going to prove that I'm stronger than her." *"I must be stronger than my mother. Weak women are failures."*

- Perhaps you believe that eating is your only source of pleasure but you refuse to let it make you gain weight: "My life is so disappointing. My only pleasure is eating; but I can't let myself gain weight because fat people are disgusting." *"I deserve pleasure but I don't want to pay the consequences."*

- Perhaps you believe that you won't be loved if you aren't perfect: "I will deserve to be loved only if I am thin." "People will think that I'm worthless if I'm not a size 5." "Being perfect is the only way to please others. I can be perfect by refusing to eat or by maintaining the perfect weight." "Not everyone can run 15 miles a day. Because I'm perfect in my exercising, people will admire me." *"I have to be perfect."*

- Perhaps you believe that the only way you can control your life is to exercise radical control over your eating: "My parents fight all the time—their bickering drives me crazy and they never stop. I can't control them, but I can control this." "The people in my father's church are so mean to him. I'll show them how angry I am and starve myself." *"Life is so chaotic, I must be in control."*

- Perhaps you believe that your disorder will give you more power over your family and the circumstances of your life: "If they think that I'm sick, then they'll feel sorry for me and be more sensitive to my wants." *"I deserve attention."*

If you compulsively overeat (but don't purge or starve yourself), you might have some of the following thoughts:

- Perhaps you believe that you deserve to give yourself pleasure through food because no one loves you in the ways you want to be loved: "No one really cares for me or understands me. Food is a true comfort to me." *"I deserve comfort and love."*

- Perhaps you're filled with self-loathing (a sinful self-focus): "No one loves me. I'm ugly. I'll eat this food because I deserve to be fat." *"I feel unloved. I deserve to be ugly."*

- Perhaps you've never learned to handle sinful emotions in a godly way: "I feel so angry/depressed/fearful. Eating is the only way that I can handle negative emotions." "I'm so angry at my boss, but I'm afraid to confront him. I deserve to eat this food instead." "I'm so depressed. When I feel this way I comfort myself with ice cream." "I'm so afraid. I have to eat now because I don't know what tomorrow will hold." *"I deserve to eat when I'm emotionally upset."*

- Perhaps you believe that you have to be perfect and overeating is the only way for you to rebel: "Everyone expects so much of me. Overeating is the only area of my life that I can safely and cheaply show them that I don't care what they think." *"I can't be perfect, so I'll show them that I don't care."*

Can you see that there is no end to our ability to manufacture gods out of our own thoughts?

Identifying the Key Problem

What do you think Marlene's true problem is? What is the root problem with any life-dominating behavior? What is the fruit of it? Is it that she makes herself throw up after she binges? Indeed, it is sinful for her to do so (because she's trying to cover up her sin, violating the Sixth Commandment, and creating a savior in her own image), but I don't think that's her primary problem.

Marlene's primary problem is that she is worshiping another god—and the worship of any god but the true God *always* ends up in futility, humiliation, and destruction. This pattern is clearly seen in the history of the children of Israel as they repeatedly turned from the worship of the true God to the worship of idols. The outcome of their lapses into idolatry was *always* judgment in the form of more and more heinous idolatry, oppression by their enemies, hostility from the creation, meaninglessness, fear, despair, and death.[4] Look at how their idolatry played out in their lives: They "served their idols, *which became a snare to them*" (Psalm 106:36, emphasis added); and "In spite of all this [God's continual care for them] they still sinned, and did not believe in His wonderful works. So He brought their days to an end in futility, and their years in sudden terror" (Psalm 78:32-33).

I can imagine that those words may seem hard for you. I am not condemning you, nor am I telling you that you are without hope. No, I want to direct you to your *only* source of hope, the living God. All gluttonous behaviors are so very destructive; I must not sugarcoat the true dynamics involved. If by these words you are filled with a godly fear that cries out, "I will have no other gods before You, Lord! I will put away the gods of my own making and worship and serve only You!" then I rejoice—even if you have been made uncomfortable by what I've said.

You must understand that there is no satisfaction, no ultimate peace or joy in idolatry. It might seem satisfying at first to eat five bags of potato chips, or to know that you can go a week without food, but after a while, that won't be enough. *The Law of Diminishing Returns is in full force in idol worship.* This behavior will grow and grow until it completely consumes you and you spend your entire life compulsively overeating, bingeing, purging, or starving. Your god has an insatiable hunger—and if you feed him, he'll grow.

Marlene's first course of action was to replace the worship of her idol with the worship of the true God. She had to confess her self-centered focus as sin—not just some inconvenient disorder.

Look back over the list of possible idolatrous thoughts on pages 173-174. What do you notice about them? Yes, each is intensely self-focused. Every thought is concentrated solely on ordering one's life to satisfy and please only one person. Even the thought that says, "I must perfectly please others" is self-focused. The person who makes herself into a doormat to try to please others does so out of self-love: "I must live to please others so that they will love me." The woman who is filled with self-loathing is that way because of an intense self-love: "I'm better than this. I don't deserve to be this fat. I hate that I do this to myself. I deserve for people to love me. I'll show them that I don't care and can eat whatever I want. They should love me for who I am inside." Can you see why such thinking is sinful?

Thinking Upon What Is True

For Marlene to change, she must first redirect her thoughts. Remember our "Think on These Things" chart? (see Appendix F). She must measure the truthfulness of her thought, "*I must be thinner than my sisters,*" by God's criteria:

- Is it true that she will attain peace and joy only by being thinner than her sisters? Is it true that God wants her to pursue this goal? Is it true that her appearance will help her in her goal to be conformed to the image of Christ?

- She must ask herself if her thoughts are honorable to her King. Is leaning over a toilet and cramming a spoon down her throat so that she can throw up a behavior that demonstrates that she believes that her Father is also King of the universe and worthy of all praise? She knows that if she pursues her idolatrous thoughts about thinness, this is where she will end up.

- Do her thoughts reflect the righteousness that Christ has purchased for her, or are they part of the way she thought before she knew Him?

- Are her thoughts pure? Would she be ashamed for other believers to know that she is consumed with comparing her body to those of her sisters?

- Is her competition with her sisters truly lovely? Would it draw others to Christ? Is she seeking to establish her own beauty so that she can be worshiped, or is she seeking to reflect Christ's beauty so He will be worshiped?

- Does pursuing this goal fill her heart with faith in Christ, or does it demonstrate a basic unbelief in the goodness, wisdom, might, and love of God?

- Are her thoughts morally excellent? Do they cause her to reflect more and more the holiness of God? If an unbeliever could see into her heart, would he or she be convicted of his or her sinfulness and drawn to worship the true God?

- Does her pursuit of this god (even on the days that she thinks she did well, thereby establishing her own brand of self-righteousness) fill her heart with the praises of God?

Putting God Before Food

Do you see why the first order of business for Marlene involved the putting away of her old gods and the renewing of her mind? If you are like Marlene, you will have to fight the fight of faith to put these gods away. They were strong in her life and may be in yours, as well. You may experience fear as you seek to change. Marlene thought, *If I stop thinking this way then I'll gain weight! I can't stand that thought! It's like a vacuum that is sucking me into a black abyss of fat and loss of personhood.* Marlene had to recognize that her god lied to her and that instead of falling into a black abyss, she would be *falling into her loving Father's arms.* You must remember that sin is deceptive—don't listen to the sulphurous fumings of your heart. Rather, listen to, believe, and obey God's Word.

Ask yourself this question: "What is the worst thing that could possibly happen if I gave up these idols?" After you answer this question, ask yourself another one: "Will that stop me from reaching my goal of being pleasing to God?" Remember, you want to keep your eyes on God's goal. What would happen if you gave up your habitual practice of self-starvation? And would that stop you from being pleasing to God? What would happen if you ran to Christ, instead of the refrigerator, to save you from your trouble?

Loving God and Your Neighbor

As you wrestle through these issues—and I mean *wrestle*—you'll also have to work on rethinking the laws that you have made for yourself. You'll have to seek, through the study of God's Word, to embrace His law rather than your own.

One measurement you can use to judge the rightness of your "laws" is this: Do my laws (whatever they are) help me to love God with my whole heart, soul, mind, and strength? And to love my neighbor as myself? Marlene's law, *"Thou shalt exercise off 500 calories every day,"* did not cause her love for God to grow and frequently caused her to sin against the command to love her neighbor—in this case, her neighbors were the members of her family, who were often ignored and harangued by her because she was so exhausted all the time and consumed with how many calories she had eaten. Marlene's life was so self-focused, so filled with self-love that she had little time left over for the love of God or her neighbor.

What are your laws? Are they affecting your love for God and others? A very valuable exercise for you would be to compare your laws with God's standards for godly eating. I've outlined them for you generally throughout this entire book, and specifically in the D-I-S-C-I-P-L-I-N-E-D Eating questions. Measure your laws according to those standards. When your heart accuses you, saying that you have "sinned" because you failed to obey one of your *own* laws, challenge the thought with what God says in His Word. Review each of the D-I-S-C-I-P-L-I-N-E-D Eating verses. Have you truly sinned against God, or have you sinned against your idol? If you discover that you feel guilt because you have transgressed laws of your own making, ask God's forgiveness for having standards that are different from His, and seek to conform your thoughts to His. In the study questions at the end of the book, I've created a form that will help you pinpoint your personal idol(s), your idol's laws, the way that you respond when you violate these laws, and whether these laws are godly or not (see Appendix E). Feel free to make copies of this form for your personal use.

Practicing Self-Control

In addition to doing away with your underlying false gods and laws, you'll want to work on practicing self-control. If you are anorexic, you might think that you already are self-controlled. You may be surprised to find that's actually not the case. A slavish devotion to starving one's self is just as self-indulgent, just as self-focused, just as out-of-control as the compulsive eater's binge. You'll want to replace that slavish devotion with the self-control of living to please God by eating in a way that demonstrates true temperance—turning away from your own desires and toward Him.

If you habitually practice any of these behaviors, let me encourage you again to make an appointment with a nutritionist today. Ask her to give you a diet plan that will help you know how many calories in each food group to eat each day. If you are severely over- or underweight, please do not try to figure out what you should eat on your own. And, of course, if you are suffering from any of the physical problems that I outlined at the beginning of this chapter, you should be under the constant care of a physician.

Although it might be very embarrassing to do so, you should seek out an accountability partner to help you in this process of change. I've found that in my life I do so much better and am much more disciplined and motivated if I know that someone will be looking at my daily diary on a weekly basis. I would encourage you to contact a spiritually mature woman in your local church—a woman who can disciple and advise you. Even if she doesn't know much about your particular eating problem, if she is a strong Christian who loves God and knows His Word, you and she could go through this book together. Perhaps there are other women in your congregation who would like to join together in a group. I know that having an accountability partner would be a wonderful benefit for you—as it has been for hundreds of women before you.

Spend time now thinking about how you will handle temptations when they occur. Undoubtedly you will be tempted to fall back into your old ways of handling life's difficulties—how will you respond? May I recommend that you write a list of the steps you will take when you are tempted? You can include some of the following on it:

As soon as I find that I'm falling into sin again ...

- I'll cry out to God and ask Him to help me, remembering that He has promised to never leave me or forsake me.

- I'll focus my thoughts on His goodness and His wonderful blessings in my life.

- I'll remember that my old desires or idols have never helped me find peace or joy.

- I'll call my accountability partner and ask her for prayer.

- If possible, I'll go out for a walk or move myself away from the kitchen to another room.

- I'll remember that God is watching me and that He loves me so much that He sent His Son to die for my sin.

- I'll turn on some praise music or Scripture set to music and begin to sing and thank God for His kindness.

- I'll get out my D-I-S-C-I-P-L-I-N-E-D Eating verses and begin to go over them.

- If I have already begun to sin, I'll stop and repent. I'll remember that I don't have to continue on just because I've started. I'm not striving for perfection, and if I stop now, I know that God will be pleased.

Are you beginning to think of other steps you can include in your contingency plan? If you prayerfully ask God for wisdom, He'll give it to you.

A War You Can Win!

Remember that Paul referred to self-control as the "beating under of his body." That is the kind of fight that you will face. If you are bulimic, you will have to stop yourself from bingeing or purging; if you are anorexic, you will have to force yourself to eat in a measured, disciplined manner. If you compulsively overeat, you'll have to begin to put on habits of temperate eating. The first few times that you step into the ring, you might find yourself a little bloodied at the end of the round; but if you keep fighting, you'll soon find yourself standing at the bell. That's because, if you are seeking to please God, He'll be in your corner!

Remember what we said earlier about patience and practice? Even if you begin today to put off your false gods, you'll still have to struggle with the residual habits you have developed over the years. These are habits both of thought and action. Don't give up in despair. You have a wonderful Father who knows your frailties. This isn't an excuse to sin—no, it's an *encouragement* that God will continue to work with you, even in your imperfection.

Turn your whole heart to Him—embrace what God declares about Himself: "There is no other God besides Me, a righteous God and a Savior; there is none except Me. *Turn to Me, and be saved*, all the ends of the earth; for I am God, and there is no other" (Isaiah 45:2122, emphasis added).

Turn to Him today . . . He can save you; He can make you whole. Your own thoughts about how to make your life livable will not bring the comfort, peace, or joy you long for. Only God can bring true fulfillment—and He's waiting now for you to turn with your whole heart to Him. Will you do that today?

12

CROSSING THE FINISH LINE

"You have need of endurance, so that when you have
done the will of God, you may receive
what was promised."

—HEBREWS 10:36

*W*ell, we've finally made it—our final chapter! My prayer is that this book has encouraged you, given you hope, and spurred you to begin growing toward learning more and more about how to please the Lord. In the course of reading, you may have already been tempted to forget the whole matter of godly eating habits in favor of something simpler, quicker, more glitzy. May I encourage you to resist this temptation? I know from my own experience and counseling others that reshaping our thoughts and attitudes is a vital part of bringing positive change to our eating habits. Remember again that our goal isn't merely weight loss (or gain), but rather a heart and life that reflects the great goodness of our heavenly Father.

I've tried to warn and encourage you all along that this won't be an easy process. Let's look at a few verses and let me come alongside you, as your friend, with some heartfelt thoughts.

Learning How to Please God

I've been married for almost 25 years—whew! You know, I say that and I can hardly believe it! During that time, both my husband and I have done a lot of learning. I've tried to learn how to please him, learn what things he really enjoys, what things irritate him. I think that one of the reasons that the first few years of marriage are so difficult is because each partner is just beginning to learn how to make their spouse happy (and because they are awakening to the fact that their spouse doesn't really know how to do that in return yet). All that I do for my husband is done because I desire to please him, because I'm commanded to do so,[1] and also because I know that when I make him happy, I'm also making myself happy in the process.

The Similarities

Let's look at the similarities and differences in learning to please God and learning to please my spouse. Learning to please God is similar because it is a learning process— just as it was for me and my husband over the last two decades, going on three. When you first become a believer, you just know that you love God, and that's about it. You're in great need of teaching available at a solid Bible-believing church so that you don't mistakenly sin against the Lord. Another similarity is that in both relationships, learning involves more than just "knowing" what you should do. It involves the process of sanctification that we've talked about so much in this book. It has taken time for me to change and to bring my heart and my habits under the guiding hand of my Father. Likewise, it has taken time for me to convince myself that I really do want to live in a way that will please my husband.

The Differences

On the other hand, learning to please God is different than learning to please my husband. For starters, everything that God wants me to know about how to please Him is written out in His Word. By contrast, I usually have to try to guess what my husband would like—perhaps he isn't telling me, perhaps I misunderstand. Maybe I think he's in the mood for spaghetti when he really wants tacos, or maybe I think that he's tired and wants to stay home when in fact he's just dying to go to a ball game. But, with God, there's no need for second-guessing. I can gain knowledge about how to please God through the diligent study of His Word. Are you feeding upon God's Word daily so that you can better know how to please Him?

Another reason that pleasing God is different is because the Lord knows my heart. Although I might fail outwardly in serving Him, He does see my motives and intentions and blesses me when I'm trying to do right but not quite making it. I rest and rejoice in that knowledge. I can also rejoice in the knowledge that God is very familiar with my frailties and has sent the Holy Spirit to reside in me and accomplish His good pleasure.

The Blessings of Pleasing God

I rejoice because everything God asks me to do is good and, ultimately, always results in blessings. A husband might be sinfully self-centered or demanding, but God never is. As I seek to obey Him, to learn what pleases Him, it always results in an outpouring of His life in me. Consider these promises to those who persevere in pleasing Him, noting particularly the words that are emphasized:

- "You shall keep My statutes and My judgments, *by which a man may live if he does them;* I am the LORD" (Leviticus 18:5).

- "I call heaven and earth to witness against you today, that I have set before you life and death, the blessing and the curse. *So choose life in order that you may live,* you and your descendants, by loving the LORD your God, by obeying His voice, and by holding fast to Him; *for this is your life and the length of your days . . .*" (Deuteronomy 30:19-20).

- *"Length of days and years of life, and peace* they will add to you" (Proverbs 3:2).

- *"Godliness actually is a means of great gain,* when accompanied by contentment" (1 Timothy 6:6).

Aren't those wonderful promises? You know, God would be just if He demanded your obedience without offering you a reward. But He's so good and kind that He offers you life, blessings, longevity, peace, and great gain when you seek to please Him.

The Process of Pleasing God

Paul talks about pleasing the Lord in Ephesians 5:8-10: "Walk as children of light (for the fruit of the light consists in all goodness and righteousness and truth), *trying to learn what is pleasing to the Lord*" (emphasis added). Paul recognizes that there is a learning deficiency among all the children of light. We all have HDD—Holiness Deficit Disorder. We are to have streams of goodness, righteousness, and truth flowing out of our lives, but that isn't enough. These characteristics need to be honed, refined, purified. We need to learn, even in the midst of doing good, just how to please Him. Like all learning, this involves a testing—a considering of one's actions and then a testing of them against Scripture.

For example, I might believe that I can eat anything I want, whenever I want it, just as long as I'm hungry for it. That seems plausible to me; it seems right in my own eyes.[2]

But, as we have already discovered, there are other biblical criteria aside from desire and hunger that should guide my food choices. I have to take all of my ideas, all of my imaginations, and evaluate them by Scripture. That's the only way I can know whether my eating is pleasing to God or not. It's interesting, but I find that my natural way of doing things is almost always at odds with God's way. That's okay as long as I recognize that I need to learn more and to become more obedient.

This process of learning to please God is ongoing. It won't be fully accomplished until we're in heaven and all of the impediments to our sanctification are removed. I long for that day, don't you? Just to hear Him say, "Well done, good and faithful servant." I know that without His great grace and mercy, I would never hear Him say that. I'm not good, and I'm rarely as faithful as I should be. But I trust that He will change me and teach me how to glorify Him.

Paul also talks about pleasing God in Colossians 1:9-12:

> We have not ceased to pray for you and to ask that you may be filled with the knowledge of His will in all spiritual wisdom and understanding, *so that you may walk in a manner worthy of the Lord, to please Him in all respects*, bearing fruit in every good work and increasing in the knowledge of God; strengthened with all power, according to His glorious might, for the attaining of all steadfastness and patience; joyously giving thanks to the Father, who has qualified us to share in the inheritance of the saints in light (emphasis added).

What was Paul's prayer for these believers? He was praying that they would have the knowledge and the resultant wisdom and understanding that they needed—why?—so that they would walk in a manner that was glorifying and pleasing to God. He knew that we don't automatically receive that knowledge when we become believers—he longed that every Christian would have it, though. He knew that as we grow in our understanding of how to please God that we will bear fruit, be strengthened by His power, and be filled to overflowing with joy and thanksgiving.

Now, that's exactly what I'm praying that God will do in you. I recognize that you can't do this on your own, and that's why you need His "glorious might." But I am also sincerely and fervently hoping that you'll persevere in your quest to please Him in your eating habits. You might not have instantaneous results—or, perhaps you will—but remember, the point isn't mere outward change. It is a change of heart.

I've tried as best I can to lay out before you a detailed and concise outline of what I believe to be principles for godly eating. I hope that you are excited about the possibility that your eating might reflect the redemption He purchased for you. If you believe that this is what the Bible teaches about eating, you'll need to make a commitment now that you won't give up until you've reached your goal. Yes, you will be tempted to quit, to try something different, but remember that God is more interested in your change than even you are. You *can* reflect His glory!

"Do not fear, for I am with you; do not anxiously look about you, for I am your God. I will strengthen you, surely I will help you, surely I will uphold you with My righteous right hand" (Isaiah 41:10). When you're sorely tempted to give up, when you think it just isn't worth it, when you start to believe the lie that you'll never change, remember this verse. If you are His child, He promises that He is with you—that He will strengthen, help, and uphold you. Don't spend time looking at the results someone else might be having with the latest fad diet. Don't worry that you're beyond God's help. According to Isaiah 41:10, He's holding you up with His hand!

Just imagine crossing the street with a little three-year-old. Although those sweet little fingers are grasping your hand, you aren't relying on them to hang on to you. No, you hold his whole hand (and part of his arm) in your grip, and nothing will pry your fingers loose. That's a picture of what your heavenly Father is doing with you. He's holding onto you. And He's stronger than you could ever imagine. To put it in Jesus' words, "no one is able to snatch [His sheep] out of the Father's hand" (John 10:29)—no, not even you. He's going to get His children across the street without any accidents.

The Struggle in Pleasing God

Are you struggling? Remember that discipline—and learning to be disciplined—is unpleasant at first. "All discipline for the moment seems not to be joyful, but sorrowful; yet to those who have been trained by it, afterwards it yields the peaceful fruit of righteousness" (Hebrews 12:11). The discipline that God brings to us is meant for a purpose: to enable us to produce the "peaceful fruit of righteousness." The fruit grown by God's loving instruction in the garden of our heart is called righteousness. This righteousness, or godly living, is a "peaceful fruit" because living a righteous life will always produce a peace in your heart that will overwhelm you. This harvest is so delicious, so satisfying—you'll be able to feast on it eternally.

It seems to me that we live in a time in which people believe that struggles or pain of any sort is evil. Some Christians even believe that it is a lack of faith that causes people to suffer. I don't believe this. I believe that God's discipline is a mark that we belong to Him. In fact, later in Hebrews we read that if you aren't disciplined by Him, you're not His child.

As you seek God's discipline in your life, including learning how to eat in a self-controlled manner, you'll discover that this is very painful in some ways. I chaff against having to ask myself the D-I-S-C-I-P-L-I-N-E-D Eating questions. I don't like it when God points out my hypocrisy, unbelief, or rebellion. It is painful. But, I've already experienced the reward of such discipline—a life overflowing with the peaceful fruit of righteousness.

Remember that as you continue on in your struggle to please God in your eating, the most lovely, delicious fruit will begin to flow from your life. It will refresh everyone around you and bring glory to Him. We modern Christians must seek to regain the truth that "it is by God's discipline that Christians are made. He who does not bear the yoke of Christ is good for nothing to others, and never gains rest to his own soul."[3]

Finishing the Course

I enjoy going to the gym. I really like attending my step classes, but I've learned something over the years. I've learned that although I want to exercise and look forward to going, once I'm at about the 35-minute mark, I begin wondering why I'm there. I can't believe that I have to pay for the privilege of sweating, breathing hard, and tiring my muscles. I pay for this?! They ought to pay *me!* However, once the class is over, when I'm stretching out on the floor after I've persevered, I'm glad that I went.

In some small way, that's what the Christian life of discipline is like. You're in a race. For most of us this race is a marathon rather than a sprint. The thought of running a marathon may seem enticing to some people (it never has to me). But I know that even long-distance runners hit a wall and have to force themselves to go on—when everything within them is screaming for them to stop. At this wall, finishing the race seems impossible. The temptation to quit becomes great. So that we won't succumb to that temptation, let's look at a couple of verses that can offer us tremendous encouragement.

In 1 Corinthians 9:24, right after Paul talks about disciplining the body, he says, "Do you not know that those who run in a race all run, but only one receives the prize? Run in such a way that you may win." Paul wants you to ask yourself, "Why bother running if I'm not out to win?" Or, to be more specific, why bother starting to learn godly eating habits if you aren't out to succeed? And if you really want to succeed, you'll have to persevere. You might have the fastest start ever timed in the Boston Marathon, but if you don't make it all the way to the finish line, no one will remember your good start. Recognize that you're in this race for the long haul. Set your sights on nothing less than success. May our God help each of us to be zealous to please Him! Not zealous to gain (or lose) weight, but zealous to please Him.

Running with Endurance

Since we have such a huge crowd of men of faith watching us from the grandstands, let us strip off anything that slows us down or holds us back, and especially those sins that wrap themselves so tightly around our feet and trip us up; and let us run with patience the particular race that God has set before us. Keep your eyes on Jesus, our leader and instructor. He was willing to die a shameful death on the cross because of the joy he knew would be his afterwards; and now he sits in the place of honor by the throne of God. If you want to keep from becoming fainthearted and weary, think about his patience as sinful men did such terrible things to him (Hebrews 12:1-3 TLB).

What a precious passage this is to those of us who are laboring in the race! Let's look at it phrase by phrase and allow our hearts to be cheered:

"...a huge crowd of men of faith watching us from the grandstands..."

Hebrews 11 describes the saints who have gone before us—and just in case we think that they are so far above us that they wouldn't be involved in our struggle, this verse tells us that they are watching us . . . and I love the liberty that the writers of The Living Bible took in saying that they're in "the grandstands." It paints the picture that they are not only watching, but they are also cheering us on. "You can make it," Moses shouts. "I was in the desert for 40 years and I know what it's like to think that you'll never make it, but you can cross over into your promised land!" "Keep going," cheers Sarah. "I didn't believe that God could give me a son, but He was faithful, even when I wasn't. You can make it; God will keep His promise to you!" "Hang in there!" cries Rahab. "I thought that my sinful past would exclude me from His family. But I was wrong. God is more merciful than you can ever imagine!" Do you hear them calling to you? If that's not enough, remember that both your Savior and the Holy Spirit are interceding, right now, for you.

> *"Let us strip off anything that slows us down or holds us back, and especially those sins that wrap themselves so tightly around our feet and trip us up."*

I hope that now you are able to identify the sins and inclinations of your heart that trip you up. As you continue to faithfully ask yourself the D-I-S-C-I-P-L-I-N-E-D Eating questions, you'll gain more and more insight. When you discover a particular area of weakness, strip it off! Don't coddle it or think about how comfy it is. Remember what it will do: Just when you start hitting your pace and feeling strong, down you'll go! And then, when you're laying there on the sidewalk in pain, you'll say, "How foolish I was not to strip this off while I had chance!"

> *". . . let us run with patience the particular race that God has set before us."*

There it is again—the word "patience." A marathon runner knows the value of patience—it's going to take time and effort to get to the finish line. Whenever you discover that you're feeling impatient, just ask yourself what it is that you would rather be doing than running toward your heavenly Father.

This race won't last forever. In the grand scheme of eternity, it is like the point of a pin, or as James puts it, "you are just a vapor [a mist, smoke] that appears for a little while and then vanishes away" (James 4:14). You'll have all of eternity to relax, rest, and rejoice in His presence.

There's one additional point I'd like to mention. This is the race that God has chosen specifically for *you*. I've often wished that I had some other race, some other problem, instead of this one. But remember, He's the great Teacher and you and I are the students. He knows just what we need to learn and how that learning will fit into His grand plan for the ages.

> *"Keep your eyes on Jesus, our leader and instructor. He was willing to die a shameful death on the cross because of the joy he knew would be his afterwards; and now he sits in the place of honor by the throne of God."*

As you run, don't look at yourself, those running by you, those falling out of the race, or even to the ground. No, keep your eyes glued upon Jesus, who ran before you towards the joy of pleasing His Father. Think about what He went through for your sake—it will make your struggle seem minuscule. Think about the scourging, the mocking, the humiliation, the pain of the nails in His hands and feet, the spear in His side. He persevered through all these things for you. And now, He's obtained the joy, and because He made it, you can be certain that you will make it, too. Remember who is holding your hand!

> *"If you want to keep from becoming fainthearted and weary, think about his patience as sinful men did such terrible things to him."*

Well, there it is again—"patience." You haven't endured anything even close to what Jesus endured for you. When you're tired and weary, when you feel discouraged and afraid, remember the patience He exercised while men were abusing Him—all for you. If He would do that, is there anything that He will withhold from you as you seek the joy of pleasing His Father? "He who did not spare His own Son, but delivered Him up for us all, how will He not also with Him freely give us all things?" (Romans 8:32).

The Rewards in Pleasing God

Yes, you *can* make it! You can change, and God will be glorified! If you haven't done so already, take time now to pray that God will help you to be filled with patience and endurance. I believe that the principles I've outlined here for you are biblical. Because these principles are God's plan, I have strong hope that God desires for you to be successful in this program . . . not successful so your vanity or pride will be fed, but so that your life will cause Him joy.

Some of us have a shorter race to run than others. Some of us have more sins that we need to strip off in order to run freely. Some of us are already fainthearted and weary. But no matter where you are in this race, I am thoroughly convinced that if you are His, God will bring you to the place where you can say, "I hunger and thirst, my Lord, only for You. I long for my entire being—my heart, my mind, my emotions, my body—to glorify You and bring You joy. I put aside the meager pleasures of this life, especially those that I find in eating, and desire only You. You are my chief joy, my wonderful Shepherd. You've spread a banqueting table before me and I anxiously await the time when I'll be there, with You, my Husband, rejoicing as Your bride. Until then, I pledge to patiently run towards You, shunning anything that would keep me from my goal, cloud my sight, or defile my wedding dress. Keep me in Your loving arms, my Father. I'm on my way home."

I heard, as it were, the voice of a great multitude and as the sound of many waters and as the sound of mighty peals of thunder, saying, "Hallelujah! For the Lord our God, the Almighty, reigns. Let us rejoice and be glad and give the glory to Him, for the marriage of the Lamb has come and His bride has made herself ready." And it was given to her to clothe herself in fine linen, bright and clean; for the fine linen is the righteous acts of the saints. And he said to me, "Write, *'Blessed are those who are invited to the marriage supper of the Lamb.'*" And he said to me, "These are true words of God" (Revelation 19:6-9, emphasis added).

PRACTICAL STEPS FOR FURTHER STUDY

*I*n the following pages you'll find direction for further study. If you are working with an accountability partner, or in a study group, these directions and questions can be used for group work. I recommend that you read each chapter *before* you work on the questions, rather than just flipping through the pages to look up the answers without really digesting the material.

The questions and verses that I've presented here are designed to help stimulate your thinking. Most of the questions expand on concepts that I've included in the chapters, but some of them reflect nuances not mentioned previously. Try to make an effort to not rush through what you learn. Rather, meditate on each truth that is presented, looking for ways to incorporate it into your own life.

If you complete one chapter of this book each week, you'll be finished in three months. I think that is preferable to quickly reading the whole book in a few days. Take time to grow in your understanding and practice of the D-I-S-C-I-P-L-I-N-E-D Eating questions. Fill out your daily diary and learn about your own areas of weakness and God's great strength. If you are looking to please your Father in the area of your eating, then patiently and diligently seek to put on each of the principles I've presented.

Weighing Yourself

I'd like to add a special word about weighing yourself. If you are slavishly bound to the scale—if what you weigh determines your peace and joy for the day—then you'd better get rid of your scale. At the very least, you should commit to *not* weighing yourself between accountability meetings, or if you aren't meeting with anyone, perhaps once per month would be adequate. If you are seriously under- or overweight, you can measure your weight to see how you're progressing, but you must remember that your goal *is not* merely the gain or loss of weight (although that might result as you learn to eat properly). Your goal is to learn to please God in every aspect of your life, including your eating. How much you weigh may or may not be an accurate measurement of that. If you are resisting the temptation to follow a fad diet, your loss or gain will be very gradual, and if you're looking for instant results and weighing yourself five times a day, you'll get discouraged very quickly.

LOVE
*to*EAT

HATE
*to*EAT

CHAPTER 1

FROM HEARTACHE TO A
SENSE OF PURPOSE

1. In what ways are your eating patterns similar to either Marsha's, Angela's, or mine? How long have you struggled with such eating patterns?

2. Would you say that you are a person who both loves and hates to eat? Have you experienced the "tyranny of food"? In what ways? Why have you decided to work on your problem now?

3. What do you think God's purpose in your life is? Would you agree that your purpose is to glorify and enjoy Him? Why or why not?

4. What does the word *glorify* mean? What would it mean to you *personally* to glorify God? How would glorifying God in your eating habits change the way that you normally think about food?

5. Do you think about God as someone you can enjoy? List five characteristics of God that you most enjoy:

   a.

   b.

   c.

   d.

   e.

Write a prayer of praise and commitment. Start with the above list of the five characteristics that you most enjoy about God. Also include in it both your fears and your desires to glorify God through your eating:

CHAPTER 2

THE CHANGE GOD DESIRES

1. What does 2 Timothy 3:16-17 teach about the purpose and power of the Bible? Is this the way that you have thought about Scripture?

2. What change is God most interested in accomplishing in you? What verses in the book of Romans affirm this? Write out these verses here:

3. Do you really believe that God can change you? Why or
    why not? Read 2 Thessalonians 2:13. Why has God
    chosen you? What specific thought or deeds do you
    think that God wants to change in you in the upcoming
    weeks? How about months?

4. Do you see yourself as a lush, green willow that is
    drinking deeply of God's grace and mercy? Do you
    believe that you can produce fruit from your life that
    will glorify Him? What does the fact that these things
    can be true in your life mean to you?

5. Prayerfully read over the list of the attributes of God on
    pages 30-34. Which ones are the most meaningful to
    you? Which ones are the most difficult for you to
    understand? Spend time in prayer now, asking God to
    reveal Himself to you more and more as you progress
    through this study. Thank Him for His wonderful char-
    acter. Rejoice in the truth that God has chosen *you*
    personally and that it's His pleasure to change you.

CHAPTER 3

MIRROR, MIRROR, IN MY HEART

1. Describe your idea of the "perfect" woman.

2. Do you believe that a woman must be thin or outwardly beautiful in order to be happy? Why or why not? Does the way you live your life agree with your answer?

3. Do you habitually compare your figure to the figures of other women? Are you competitive, jealous, despairing, or anxious about how you measure up? Do you judge others by their appearance?

4. What does God say about beauty from 1 Peter 3:3-4? How do His thoughts compare with yours? How can you put on the kind of beauty that He calls "precious"?

5. What thoughts went through your mind when you read the statement that thinness is not something that God commands?

6. What does it mean to "fear God"? How would this chapter's concept of fearing God differ from any previous concept you might have had?

Think about the wealth, wisdom, and power of your heavenly Father. Thank Him now that He's your Father (there is no one else like Him!) and that He has committed all His resources and power to help you in your desire to please Him.

LOVE *to* EAT

HATE *to* EAT

C H A P T E R   4

WE ARE GOD'S TEMPLE

1. List two reasons why you should be concerned about caring for your body. Is caring for your body a high priority in your life? Why or why not?

2. Write out Psalm 139:13-14. Write out a prayer of thanks for God's creation of you—specifically naming the parts of your body that you are most unhappy with (like I do with my arms).

3. List any illnesses or frailties that you have had. How have these frailties taught you to rely on God? How has God used them to bless others?

4. How does the knowledge that God indwells you influence your thoughts about your body? Does the knowledge that you are His temple change your attitude or behavior in any way? How?

5. Does the Sixth Commandment refer only to "murder"? What else does it refer to? How should this commandment impact your eating habits? What changes do you need to make to avoid violating the Sixth Commandment?

Write a prayer of consecration as you reflect on the terribly beautiful vision of the cross. List the thoughts and behaviors that you think you should leave there as a sacrifice for Him. Rejoice in the fact that He owns you by creation and by His redemption.

CHAPTER 5

WHY WE DO
WHAT WE DO

1. Look at pages 64-66 and list the seven most common answers to the question, "Why do we do what we do?" Which ones are you most familiar with? What do these seven answers have in common? How do they square with the Bible?

2. Have you felt as if something from your past was holding you back from fully following the Lord? What might that be? After reflecting on the description of those whom God calls, do you think that you are going to be able to change? Why or why not?

3. Read James 1:13-16, then write out verse 14 in your own words. What does this verse teach about the way we sin? Who is responsible for our sin? What happens when you follow your lusts or desires? Why does James warn his readers about being deceived?

4. How can you grow in your understanding of the thoughts and intentions of your heart? Why is it important to do so?

5. What are some personal desires that you see within your own heart? (For instance: the love of independence, power, approval of others.) Do you think that your desires will ever be satisfied? Why or why not?

6. Read Psalm 73:25: "Whom have I in heaven but Thee? And besides Thee, I desire nothing on earth." Do you think about God in this way? What else do you desire besides His loving presence in your life? In light of your responses, why not write a prayer of confession and trust?

CHAPTER 6

GOD'S LIFE-CHANGING POWER

1. Write out the four biblical steps for change:
    a.
    b.
    c.
    d.

   Which one seems the most difficult? Which one seems the most confusing?

2. What was your immediate response when you first read the steps? Do you believe that God's method for change is contained in these steps? Why or why not?

3. In what ways does the Holy Spirit enable you to follow these four steps?

4. What does the Bible mean when it says that you have been "sealed until the day of redemption"? What part of that sealing activity is the most precious to you? Why does it give you hope?

5. After reading this chapter and observing how the Holy Spirit helps us, are you starting to believe that your eating habits can become godly? Write either a prayer of petition that God would encourage you to believe, or a prayer of thanks for His power working in your life.

CHAPTER 7

A RIGHT PERSPECTIVE OF FOOD

1. Why is it important to call your destructive eating habits "sin"? Have you ever thought about them in this way before? In what ways are your destructive eating habits sinful?

2. Is enjoying food sinful? Why or why not?

3. The Bible speaks frequently about feasting. What are some of the communal eating times that the Bible refers to?

4. List some beneficial habits that you have. Now list some detrimental ones. What are the blessings of the capacity to form habits? What are the curses?

5. Write out Romans 6:12-13 in your own words. Write out a prayer of commitment as I did on page 114, inserting your name and praying that you will not use the parts of your body as weapons against righteousness.

CHAPTER 8

MAKING GODLY
FOOD CHOICES

1. Is there an overriding biblical principle that can be applied to your eating habits? What is it? Where in the Bible do we find mention of this principle?

2. Write out the **D-I-S-C-I-P-L-I-N-E-D** Eating questions (you can look them up in Appendix A if you haven't memorized them yet):

D

I

S

C

I

P

L

I

N

E

D

E

3. Which one of the D-I-S-C-I-P-L-I-N-E-D Eating questions is the most meaningful to you? Which area do you think you'll have the most trouble with? Why?

4. Do you think that you'll need to use a preplanned eating program? Which one will you use (or would you like to use)? What steps do you need to take to begin to implement it now?

5. Have you begun to use the daily diary? If yes, have you begun to see any areas where you consistently succeed? What areas do you need to grow in? How are you doing with your spiritual disciplines? Are you praying and reading the Word?

Remember that even though this process might seem foreign to you, God can help you establish new habits. If you have already begun to use the daily diary and are struggling with it, why not ask God for renewed strength now? In a prayer of consecration, look to Him to strengthen, establish, and encourage you in your struggles.

CHAPTER 9

FOOD AND YOUR THOUGHT LIFE

1. Your thoughts, emotions, and behaviors are closely entwined. In light of the diagrams on page 136, are you beginning to understand some steps you can take to control your emotions and your thoughts? What are they?

2. Write out Philippians 4:8. Which of the characteristics of godly thinking do you have the most difficulty with? Why? Which ones are easiest for you? Why?

3. Do you see any correlation between your habitual thought patterns and your habitual eating patterns? How would you describe the correlation?

4. What does "let your mind dwell on these things" mean?

5. What do you think Job meant when he said, "I have treasured the words of His mouth more than my necessary food"? (Job 23:12).

Look again at the *Think on These Things* grid in Appendix E. Ask the Lord to help you learn to train your thoughts to be pleasing to Him. Although this may seem difficult at first, remember that He is there with you, enabling your change for Him.

CHAPTER 10

PRACTICE, PRACTICE, PRACTICE

1. Can you think of any ways that God uses the abiding sin in your life?

2. Sometimes I slip into a mindset that says, "If God wants to change me, He knows where I live." Have you ever had similar thoughts? If so, can you pinpoint the error in thinking this way? Am I responsible for my change? What about God's responsibility?

3. Do you find yourself being impatient with the amount of time it's taking for you to change? Why? Do you believe that God could "zap" you if He so desired? Why do you think that He hasn't done that?

4. What is the picture that James gives of the person who hears the Word but doesn't practice it? In what ways do you sometimes act like that person?

5. Make a list of ten items that you are thankful for. Each day, during your prayer time, review this list out loud, thanking God for each item.

    a.

    b.

    c.

    d.

    e.

    f.

    g.

    h.

    i.

    j.

Encourage yourself now by going over each item for which you are thankful, and direct your heart to rejoice in God's great blessings to you.

CHAPTER 11

A WORD SPECIFICALLY FOR YOU

1. Do any of the thoughts presented on pages 173-174 function as gods for you? Which one(s)? Are you aware of any other false gods that might be present in your life? Even if you don't practice any of these life-dominating sins, you may have other idols such as, "I MUST ALWAYS HAVE A CLEAN HOUSE," "I MUST HAVE A GODLY HUSBAND," "I DESERVE RESPECT," "I DESERVE TO BE TREATED BETTER THAN THIS," or "I MUST NEVER BE ALONE."

2. On the next page you'll find a blank diagram for you to complete. Try to ascertain whether you're worshiping a false god, what that god's laws are, and how this worship makes you act. It is quite common to struggle with idolatry even when you love God—to fluctuate between your idolatry and the worship of the living God, and to have very mixed desires. A self-centered desire to be thin, for instance, might also be confused with a godly desire to be self-disciplined and a good

witness. In time you'll grow in your ability to judge whether you're serving God or your idol as you observe the behavior that flows from your desire. For instance, if your desire is truly to be self-disciplined for God's glory, then you won't find yourself purging or sinning in any other way when you fail. Rather, you'll confess your sin to the Lord you are seeking to please and move on in repentance.

Your god: Your god's laws:

_____   _____

                                 _____

                                 _____

Your practices:

_____

_____

_____

_____

_____

3. Let's look at how Marlene changed her worship and service:

THE LIVING GOD   HIS LAWS:
                                  D-I-S-C-I-P-L-I-N-E-D Eating

Doing all to the glory of God.

Marlene transgresses God's law (sins), so she
humbly asks for His forgiveness and recommits to
serve only Him; she seeks patiently to please only Him
and realizes that He has promised to forgive her, to
change her, and to remake her into His image, so she . . .

Joyfully gives thanks for His grace in her life,
puts off trying to prove that she's perfect, and
rejoices in the righteousness of Christ alone.
When she sees her sisters, she's filled with love and
care for them and seeks ways to minister
God's grace instead of competing with them.

4. How would a change in the focus of your worship change your behavior?

5. Write out Exodus 20:1-6 in your own words. Ask God to show you the areas where you need to grow in whole-hearted devotion to Him. Remember that He already knows these things and is waiting to help and encourage you.

LOVE
*to*EAT

H*a*TE
*to*EAT

C H A P T E R 1 2

CROSSING THE
FINISH LINE

1. Since you became a Christian, what have you learned about pleasing God?

2. Write out Isaiah 41:10. What does this verse mean to you?

3. Would you like to finish the race God has given you? The race that He chooses for us can change from time to time. What race has He given you to run right now? How are you doing? Are you tired? Are you tripping over a specific sin? What can you do about it?

4. Read all of Hebrews 11. What were some of the races these people had to run? How do these races compare with the one you're running? How can you be encouraged by their faithfulness?

5. What does the word *patience* mean? What does it mean to you personally? What parts of the race do you need to be more patient in? How can you do that?

Take a few moments now to meditate on the things that God has taught you through this study. You may want to list them in order of their importance to you—thanking the Lord for His grace and mercy.

LOVE
to EAT
———
H*A*TE
to EAT

Appendix A

D-I-S-C-I-P-L-I-N-E-D E

Eating Questions

Doubt: Do I doubt (for whatever reason) that I can eat this food without sinning?

Idolatry: Will eating this food demonstrate a heart of idolatry (pleasure/power)?

Stumble: If I eat this food, will it cause some weaker Christian to stumble?

Covet: Am I eating this food because I saw someone else with it and I'm coveting?

Inroad: If I eat this food, will it create an inroad for sin in my life?

Praise: Can I eat this food with thanks and gratitude?

Life: Would eating this food harm my life or health in any way?

Illustrate: Am I modeling good eating habits for others?

No: Am I able to say no to this food, even if I know that I can eat it without sin?

Emotions: Does the desire to eat this food flow out of any sinful emotion?

Distract: Will preparing or eating this food distract me from something more profitable?

Enslaved: Will eating this food bring me under any kind of bondage?

In my eating and drinking, am I glorifying God?

LOVE
to EAT

HATE
to EAT

Appendix B

Do I **DOUBT** *that I can eat this food without sinning?*

He who doubts is condemned if he eats, because his eating is not from faith; and whatever is not from faith is sin (ROMANS 14:23).

Will eating this food demonstrate a heart of **IDOLATRY?**

You shall have no other gods before Me (EXODUS 20:3).

Will eating this cause a weaker Christian to **S**TUMBLE?

It is good not to eat meat or to drink wine, or to do anything by which your brother stumbles (ROMANS 14:21).

Am I eating this food because I am **COVETING** *it?*

You shall not covet . . . anything that belongs to your neighbor (EXODUS 20:17).

If I eat this food, will it create an **INROAD** *for sin in my life?*

Put on the Lord Jesus Christ, and make no provision for the flesh in regards to its lusts (ROMANS 13:14).

Can I eat this food with **P**RAISE *and gratitude?*

Everything created by God is good, and nothing is to be rejected, if it is received with gratitude (1 TIMOTHY 4:4).

Would eating this food harm my **LIFE** *or health in any way?*

You shall not murder (EXODUS 20:13).

Am I **ILLUSTRATING** *good eating habits for others?*

Show yourself an example of those who believe (1 TIMOTHY 4:12).

Am I able to just say **NO?**

I buffet my body and make it my slave, lest possibly, after I have preached to others, I myself should be disqualified (1 CORINTHIANS 9:27).

Does my desire to eat this flow out of any sinful **EMOTIONS?**

If you do well, will not your countenance be lifted up? And if you do not do well, sin is crouching at the door; and its desire is for you, but you must master it (GENESIS 4:7).

Will eating or preparing this food **D**ISTRACT *me from something better?*

Martha, Martha, you are worried and bothered about so many things; but only a few are really necessary, really only one, for Mary has chosen the good part, which shall not be taken away from her (LUKE 10:41-42).

Will eating this food **E**NSLAVE *me in any way?*

All things are lawful for me, but not all things are profitable. All things are lawful for me, but I will not be mastered by anything (1 CORINTHIANS 6:12).

LOVE
to EAT

H*a*TE
to EAT

Appendix C

Daily Diary

MONDAY	D	TUESDAY	D	WEDNESDAY	D
Meats		Meats		Meats	
Grains		Grains		Grains	
Fruits		Fruits		Fruits	
Vegetables		Vegetables		Vegetables	
Dairy		Dairy		Dairy	
Other		Other		Other	
WATER ☐ ☐ ☐		WATER ☐ ☐ ☐		WATER ☐ ☐ ☐	
Cal/Fat Total		Cal/Fat Total		Cal/Fat Total	
Prayer Time		Prayer Time		Prayer Time	
Bible Chpts		Bible Chpts		Bible Chpts	
Exercise		Exercise		Exercise	
Victories:		Victories:		Victories:	
Needed Growth:		Needed Growth:		Needed Growth:	

Daily Diary

THURSDAY	D	FRIDAY	D	SATURDAY	D	SUNDAY	D
Meats		Meats		Meats		Meats	
Grains		Grains		Grains		Grains	
Fruits		Fruits		Fruits		Fruits	
Vegetables		Vegetables		Vegetables		Vegetables	
Dairy		Dairy		Dairy		Dairy	
Other		Other		Other		Other	
WATER ☐ ☐ ☐		WATER ☐ ☐ ☐		WATER ☐ ☐ ☐		WATER ☐ ☐ ☐	
Cal/Fat Total		Cal/Fat Total		Cal/Fat Total		Cal/Fat Total	
Prayer Time		Prayer Time		Prayer Time		Prayer Time	
Bible Chpts		Bible Chpts		Bible Chpts		Bible Chpts	
Exercise		Exercise		Exercise		Exercise	
Victories:		Victories:		Victories:		Victories:	
Needed Growth:		Needed Growth:		Needed Growth:		Needed Growth:	

LOVE
*to*EAT

HATE
*to*EAT

Appendix D

Daily Diary

MONDAY	D	TUESDAY	D	WEDNESDAY	D
Meats *4 oz* *Hamburger*	I	Meats *2 eggs* *½ c Tuna*		Meats *2 Hot Dogs* *3 Sl Turkey*	L
Grains *2 sl toast* *½ c noodles* *corn chips*	E	Grains *English Muffin* *2 sl bread* *2 c Pasta*		Grains *HD Bun* *2 sl bread* *Popcorn*	N
Fruits *Orange* *12 Grapes*		Fruits *No fruit*	L	Fruits *Apple* *Peach*	
Vegetables *Salad w/* *Tomatoes* *Nonfat Dressing*		Vegetables *Salad w/Pasta* *Fresh tomato* *Sauce*		Vegetables *Corn on* *the cob* *Salad (NF dressing)*	
Dairy *NF Milk*		Dairy *Yogurt*		Dairy *None*	
Other *2 Tbsp Mayo*	E	Other *1 Tbsp Mayo*		Other *Butter on* *Popcorn/Mayo*	
WATER ☒☒☐		WATER ☒☐☐		WATER ☒☒☐	
Cal/Fat Total		Cal/Fat Total		Cal/Fat Total	
Prayer Time *7:30 a.m.* Bible Chpts *John 1–2* Exercise *Walked 1 mile*		Prayer Time *7:30 a.m.* Bible Chpts *John 3–4* Exercise *None*		Prayer Time *8:00 a.m.* Bible Chpts *–0–* Exercise *Walked 1 mile*	
Victories: *Walked!* Needed Growth: *Angry – ate chips*		Victories: *Read &* *Prayed 2 days!* Needed Growth: *Exercise*		Victories: *Read* Needed Growth: *Woke up late –* *didn't read,* *overate*	

Daily Diary

THURSDAY	D	FRIDAY	D	SATURDAY	D	SUNDAY	D
Meats 2 Sl Ham 4 oz Steak	N	Meats 3 oz cheese 4 oz Halibut		Meats 2 Eggs & Hot Dogs 6 oz Hamburger	C	Meats Meatballs Chicken Breast	
Grains 2 sl bread 5 oz Potato		Grains 4 Sl bread 1 C Rice		Grains 4 Pancakes 2 HD Buns 1 HB Bun	C	Grains 1 C Pasta 1/2 C Brown Rice Popcorn	
Fruits Pear Orange Juice		Fruits Grapefruit Apple	L	Fruits None		Fruits Fruit Salad	
Vegetables 1 C Green Beans Nonfat Dressing		Vegetables Salad Nonfat Dressing Peas		Vegetables None		Vegetables Salad (NF dressing) Fresh Green Beans	
Dairy *Ice cream*	N	Dairy *Yogurt*		Dairy *Ice cream*	C	Dairy *Yogurt*	
Other *Too much* *Sour Cream*	N	Other *Marg on Rice*		Other *Toppings* *on ice cream*	C	Dairy *Butter* *on Popcorn*	
WATER ☑ ☑ ☑		WATER ☑ ☑ ☐		WATER ☑ ☑ ☑		WATER ☐ ☐ ☐	
Cal/Fat Total		Cal/Fat Total		Cal/Fat Total		Cal/Fat Total	
Prayer Time 7:30 a.m. Bible Chpts John 5-6 Exercise Walked 1 mile		Prayer Time 7:30 a.m. Bible Chpts John 7-8 Exercise Walked 2 miles!		Prayer Time 8:00 a.m. Bible Chpts -0- Exercise -0-		Prayer Time -0- Bible Chpts John 9-10 Exercise Walked 1 mile	
Victories: Read & Prayed again! Needed Growth: Should've said no to sour cream & steak		Victories: Praise God! Great Day! Needed Growth:		Victories: Needed Growth: Went to ballgame and ignored the program		Victories: One week completed Needed Growth: Consistent prayer	

LOVE
to EAT

HATE
to EAT

Appendix E

Personal Growth Sheet

	Mon	Tue	Wed	Thu	Fri	Sat	Sun	Comments/Convictions
Doubt								
Idolotry								
Stumble								
Covet								
Inroad								
Praise								
Life								
Illustrate								
No								
Emotions								
Distract								
Enslaved								

Check the **D-I-S-C-I-P-L-I-N-E-D** Eating principle that you violated on each corresponding day. At the end of the week you'll have a picture of your victories and the areas you'll need to grow in. (Thanks to Leeanna Goldschmidt & Laurie Mee for this useful tool.)

LOVE
*to*EAT

HATE
*to*EAT

Appendix F

Think on These Things

WORD	DEFINITION	ASK YOURSELF, *Is this thought . . .*
true	factual	true to the facts, or am I exaggerating or ignoring them? Is it true to the facts that I know about God? His Word? His Work? His purpose for me?
honorable	esteemed	. . . something that is beneath me as a daughter of the King? Does it keep my Father's kingship in sight?
right	righteous	. . . reflective of the righteousness that Christ has purchased for me? Or is it part of the way that I thought before I knew His love?
pure	clean	. . . something that I would be ashamed about if others knew I entertained it? Does it live up to God's standards of purity and holiness?
lovely	winsome	. . . something that would draw others to Christ? Is it sweet or bitter, beautiful or ugly?
good repute	attractive	. . . a faith-filled assessment of the situation, or does it send my heart trembling in fear away from the Lord?
moral excellence	virtue	. . . overflowing with the excellencies of Christ? Does it acknowledge His great love, mercy grace, and holiness?
praise-worthy	admirable	. . . something that would cause others to praise God if they heard it? Does it cause my heart to be filled with thanks and worship?

HOW YOU CAN KNOW IF
YOU ARE A CHRISTIAN

I'm so glad that you decided to turn to this page, way in the back of this book—and there are two reasons why I feel this way.

First of all, the truths that are contained in this book will be impossible for you to understand and follow if you aren't a Christian, and my hope is that you will come to know the joy of God-empowered change. But that really isn't the most important reason I'm glad that you decided to turn here.

I'm also so pleased that you turned to this page because I long for you to know the joy of peace with God and to have the assurance that your sins are forgiven. You see, if you've never really come to the place in your life where God opened your heart to the truth of His great love and sacrifice and your need for forgiveness, you must question whether you really are a Christian.

Many people attend church and try to live "good" lives. We certainly aren't as bad as we could be . . . and so we think that like Patrick Swayze in the movie *Ghost* it doesn't really matter if we have trusted in Christ—if we're nice and we love people, God will accept us . . . right? You know, if it were up to me, if you had to live up to my standards, I might say that we're all okay. But that's not the truth, and it isn't up to me. It's up to God . . . and His standards are different than ours. He says, "My ways are not your ways and My thoughts are not your thoughts" (see Isaiah 55:8).

The truth is that God is perfectly holy. That means that He never thinks or does anything that is inconsistent with His perfection. He is pure and without fault of any kind. That's not because He gets up every morning and says, "I'll try to be good today." No, by His very nature He is good and there's never a time when He isn't.

In addition to being perfectly holy, He is just. That means that He always sees that justice is served . . . or those who deserve punishment will always receive it in the end. Now, I know that it may not seem that way to you, looking at things like we do from an earthly perspective, but let me assure you, the Great Judge of all the earth will prevail. If God allowed people to get away with breaking His laws, then He wouldn't really be holy, would He?

In one sense, the truth of God's holiness and justice reassures us. The Hitlers of the world, even though they seemingly have escaped judgment here on earth, will stand before their Creator and will receive just what they deserve. But in another sense, God's holiness and justice should make us all uncomfortable. That's because even though we may not be as bad as we could be, we know that we all sin and God hates sin. Very simply speaking, *sin is any violation of God's perfect standards*. His standards are contained in the Bible and were summed up in the Ten Commandments in the Old Testament. Think for a moment about those commandments: Have you had any other gods in your life? Have you ever failed to revere the Lord's Day and set it apart for Him? Have you ever failed to honor those in authority over you? Have you ever taken another's life or turned your back on someone who needed your protection? Have you ever desired someone who was not your spouse? Have you ever taken anything that wasn't yours to take? Have you ever told a lie or looked at something that someone else had and wanted it for yourself?

I'm sure, if you're like me, you'll say that you've probably broken a number of God's commands at various times in your life. And there's no way you can avoid the time when one day, you will stand before God's judgment seat. And the Bible makes it clear that the wages of sin is death (see Romans 6:23). That's the punishment that sin deserves. But don't despair. If you know that you are a sinner, then there is hope for you because God is not only holy and just; He's also merciful.

God has immense love and mercy and because of this, He made a way for you and me to come to Him. He did this without compromising His holiness and justice. You see, someone had to take the punishment for your sin. Someone had to die in your place. But who could do this and still maintain God's justice?

Every person who has ever lived has sinned and is therefore disqualified from taking someone else's punishment, because they deserved punishment of their own. Only one Man could take this punishment. Only one Man was perfectly sinless and completely undeserving of punishment. That Man was Jesus Christ. Jesus Christ was both God (making Him perfectly sinless) and man (making Him suitable as our "stand-in"). The Bible teaches that because of God's love for man, He sent His Son, Jesus Christ, to die in our place. On the cross, Jesus Christ took the punishment we deserved. Thus is God's justice served and His holiness upheld. That's why the Bible teaches that "while we were yet sinners, Christ died for us" (Romans 5:8).

But that still leaves you with a problem. Perhaps as you are reading this you know that you are a sinner. You also believe that God is holy and just, and you are hoping that He is as merciful and loving as I've portrayed Him. What must you do? You must believe on Him. That means that you must believe what the Bible says about God, you, and your sin, and you must ask God to forgive you of all your sins. You can do this through prayer. There aren't any special words that you must say. In fact, the Bible says that "everyone who calls on the name of the Lord shall be saved" (Acts 2:21). You can pray to Him, asking Him to forgive your sin because of Jesus' sacrifice. You can ask Him to make you His own. The Bible says, "If we confess our sins, He is faithful and righteous to forgive us our sins and to cleanse us from all unrighteousness" (1 John 1:9). You can rest in His truthfulness.

Now, if you have become a Christian, you will want to live for Him in a way that pleases Him. In order to know how to do that, you must begin reading His Word. You should begin in the Gospel of John with the first chapter. As you read, pray that God will help you to understand.

The next thing that you should do is find a good Bible-believing church and start attending it. A Bible-believing church is one that believes in the Trinity (that the Father, the Son, and the Holy Spirit are equally one God), believes that salvation is entirely a free gift of God, practices prayer and holiness, and preaches from God's Word (without any other books added).

If you've become a Christian through the ministry of this book, I would love to know so that I can rejoice with you. Please write to me through the publisher: Harvest House Publishers, 1075 Arrowsmith, Eugene, OR, 97402. May God's richest blessings be yours as you bow humbly before His throne!

NOTES

Chapter 1—From Heartache to a Sense of Purpose

1. *The Shorter Catechism* (Carlisle, PA: The Banner of Truth Trust), p. 1.

Chapter 2—The Change God Desires

1. Hodge, A. A., *The Confession of Faith* (Carlisle, PA: The Banner of Truth Trust, 1992), p. 51.
2. Ibid., p. 50.
3. *New Unger's Bible Dictionary* (Chicago: Moody Press, 1988).
4. Ibid.
5. Christians are divided about God's desire for our happiness. Some Christians believe that God's sole purpose is to make us happy in the here and now. It seems as though they think that God's highest goal is to make us prosper materially—as though He would think that driving a Cadillac is the highest form of blessing. Those who advocate this doctrine need to take a lesson from the Bible about the folly of loving the world and the things in it. On the other hand, there are Christians who believe that God doesn't care one whit about our happiness and cringe when they hear teaching that God wants to establish our happiness. I, too, thought that way until I began to read the writings of the Puritans. They recognized that God's call was away from the misery of loving the lesser joys of the world; they also recognized that when their hearts were filled with love for Him, their happiness would overflow. In our present context, some Christians are reacting to the "prosperity message" that has been promoted by some prominent individuals, and these people seem to think that being spiritual is analogous to being miserable. I have come to believe that God delights in our happiness. Jesus came that our "joy may be made full." When our hearts are filled with joy and praise at knowing Him, He is glorified and His name is exalted. True happiness flows out of a heart that is focused on Him and comes as a result of trusting His goodness. We must delight in the things that He calls us to delight in. I believe that being happy is one of the wonderful by-products of a life dedicated to the service of Christ. God doesn't owe me anything—it's just one of His gifts to

redeem me from the sin and misery that I love and change my heart so that I delight in Him. For more on this topic, see John Piper's book *Desiring God: Confessions of a Christian Hedonist* (Portland, OR: Multnomah Press, 1988).

6. Ryle, J. C., *Holiness* (Darlington, England: Evangelical Press, 1879), p. 22.

Chapter 3—Mirror, Mirror, in My Heart

1. Although many models in magazines do look "perfect," we shouldn't forget that these photographs are usually touched up.
2. Thanks to David Powlison for his insightful article, "Your Looks: What the Voices Say and the Images Portray," *The Journal of Biblical Counseling* (1997), vol. 15, no. 2, Winter: 39-43. Copies of the journal may be ordered by contacting the Christian Counseling and Educational Foundation, 1803 East Willow Grove Avenue, Glenside, PA 19038 (215) 884-7676.
3. Powlison, p. 42. Used by permission.
4. *Clarke's Commentary* by Adam Clarke, Electronic Database. Copyright 1996 by Biblesoft.
5. Fitzpatrick, Elyse and Cornish, Carol, *Women Helping Women* (Eugene, OR: Harvest House, 1997), p. 460.
6. *Matthew Henry's Commentary on the Whole Bible:* New Modern Edition, Electronic Database (Peabody, MA: Hendrikson Publishers, 1991).
7. *Vine's Expository Dictionary of Biblical Words* (Nashville: Thomas Nelson Publishers, 1985).
8. "A Fear to Be Desired, Hosea 3:5," a sermon delivered on Thursday evening November 7, 1878 by C. H. Spurgeon at the Metropolitan Tabernacle, Newington, England, from *Spurgeon's Encyclopedia of Sermons*.

Chapter 4—We Are God's Temple

1. *Clarke's Commentary* by Adam Clarke, Electronic Database. Copyright 1996 by Biblesoft.
2. *The Westminster Standards, The Larger Catechism* (Suwanee, GA: Great Commission Publications, 1978), p. 57.
3. *Barnes' Notes* by Albert Barnes, D. D., Electronic Database. Copyright 1997 by Biblesoft.
4. Ibid., emphasis added.
5. Ibid.
6. 1 John 3:1.
7. Romans 5:8.

Chapter 5—Why We Do What We Do

1. For more information on this type of thought, see Peter Jones, *Spirit Wars* (Mukilteo, WA: WinePress, 1997).
2. Powlison, David, *Power Encounters: Reclaiming Spiritual Warfare* (Grand Rapids: Baker Books, 1995), p. 68.
3. See 1 Kings 8:39; 1 Chronicles 28:9; 1 Chronicles 29:17; Jeremiah 12:3.

4. Consider the following injunctions to self-examination: "let us examine and probe our ways, and let us return to the LORD" (Lamentations 3:40); "let a man examine himself, and so let him eat of the bread and drink of the cup" (1 Corinthians 11:28); "test yourselves to see if you are in the faith; examine yourselves! Or do you not recognize this about yourselves, that Jesus Christ is in you—unless indeed you fail the test?" (2 Corinthians 13:5).

5. It is only in the Lord that we have true understanding not only of Him, but also of ourselves: "for Thou dost light my lamp; the LORD my God illumines my darkness" (Psalm 18:28); "for with Thee is the fountain of life; in Thy light we see light" (Psalm 36:9); "Thy word is a lamp to my feet, and a light to my path" (Psalm 119:105); "the unfolding of Thy words gives light; it gives understanding to the simple" (Psalm 119:130).

6. Lewis, C. S., *Perelandra* (New York: Macmillan Publishing Company, 1944), p. 42.

7. Lewis, C.S., *The Weight of Glory and Other Addresses* quoted from John Piper, *Desiring God* (Sisters, OR: Multnomah Books, 1996).

8. See Numbers 11 for a real-time exposition of their folly.

9. *Matthew Henry's Commentary on the Whole Bible:* New Modern Edition, Electronic Database. Copyright 1991 by Hendrickson Publishers, Inc.

10. Ibid.

11. Ibid.

12. 1 John 4:8ff.

Chapter 6—God's Life-Changing Power

1. Adams, Jay E., *The Christian Counselor's Commentary: Galatians, Ephesians, Colossians, Philemon* (Hackettstown, NJ: Timeless Texts, 1994).

2. Galatians 5:22-23.

3. Romans 8:27.

Chapter 7—A Right Perspective of Food

1. David Wells, *Losing Our Virtue* (Grand Rapids: Eerdmans, 1998). As such, your personal problems either need a lawyer or a therapist.

2. Wells states that this kind of preaching is designed to accommodate our postmodern culture and is a sign of our unbelief in the power of God to regenerate modern man. We would rather be liked than preach confrontational truth. It is exactly this kind of preaching that creates such sycophant anemia in our churches and leaves believers helpless in their struggle against sin and easy bait for aberrant methods of change.

3. *Matthew Henry's Commentary on the Whole Bible:* New Modern Edition, Electronic Database. Copyright 1991 by Hendrickson Publishers, Inc.

4. Some may object that we are no longer "under the law" and therefore we can ignore the Ten Commandments. It is true that we are not under bondage to fulfill the law to try to justify ourselves and that we are not obligated to fulfill the ceremonial law. However, we are fully obligated to obey the moral law, since it is reiterated and even heightened in the New Testament.

5. *The Westminster Standards, The Larger Catechism* (Suwanee, GA: Great Commission Publications, 1978), p. 57.
6. I know that the Council at Jerusalem commanded the Gentile believers not to eat food that was sacrificed to idols, meat with the blood, or meat that had been strangled. These commands were given to promote peace between the Gentile and Jewish Christians at the time. Aside from this, I don't know of any *specific* commands about food that may be or may not be eaten given in the New Testament. Of course, the ceremonial law in the Old Testament is filled with commands regarding food, but these laws about eating were obliterated during Peter's vision about the inclusion of the Gentiles in Acts 11.
7. *Reader's Digest Oxford Complete Wordfinder* (Pleasantville, NY: The Reader's Digest Association, Inc., 1996).
8. John 8:29.
9. Matthew 4:1-4.
10. John 8:19-20.
11. Luke 12:23.
12. John 21:9-13.
13. *Nelson's Illustrated Bible Dictionary* (Nashville: Thomas Nelson Publishers, 1986).
14. C.S. Lewis, *The Screwtape Letters* (New York: MacMillan Publishing Company, Inc., 1961), pp. 76-78.
15. Jay E. Adams, *The Christian Counselor's Commentary: Romans, Philippians, I Thessalonians, II Thessalonians* (Hacketstown, NJ: Timeless Texts, 1995), pp. 51-52.
16. Romans 7 outlines Paul's struggle with remaining sinful habits and his desire to please God.

Chapter 8—Making Godly Food Choices

1. Galatians 5:19-23.
2. *Nelson's Illustrated Bible Dictionary* (Nashville: Thomas Nelson Publishers, 1986).
3. Acts 24:25. Paul spoke to Felix about righteousness, self-control, and the judgment to come.
4. Daniel 1:8.
5. Matthew 4:4.
6. The American Heart Association has a number of good, well-balanced diet books that will help you develop a nutritious eating plan including *6 Weeks to Get Out The Fat* (Random House); *365 Ways to Get Out the Fat: A Tip a Day to Keep Fat and Cholesterol Away!* (Random House); *Your Heart: An Owner's Manual* (Prentice Hall).
7. Hansen, Barbara C., Ph.D. and Roberts, Shauna S., Ph.D., *The Commonsense Guide to Weight Loss for People with Diabetes* (published by the American Diabetes Association).
8. Other factors can influence your ability to gain or lose weight. This guideline is supplied for those who aren't struggling with other physiological difficulties that stop them from losing weight in a timely fashion. The very best

course of action is for you to speak with your physician or a nutritionist about a diet specifically designed for you.

9. Hellmich, Nancy, "Aging Boomers Fight the Battle of the Bulge," *USA Today*, Health, January 4, 1996.

Chapter 9—Food and Your Thought Life

1. I'm not advocating a mind-over-matter view of illness. It's just that some illnesses, not all, are caused by sinful thinking and emotional responses.

Chapter 10—Practice, Practice, Practice

1. Psalm 144:1.
2. For a wonderful discussion on the topic of abiding sin see *Letters of John Newton* (Carlisle, PA: The Banner of Truth Trust, 1976).
3. 1 Peter 1:18.
4. I recognize that the Bible doesn't provide a list of the recommended major food groups that are necessary for maintaining good health. The Bible wasn't written to be a nutrition textbook, although information on proper eating habits *can* be gleaned from it. Because of God's common grace to man, He has allowed us to discover truth about the creation around us. Part of the truth that has been discovered is how to eat in a way that provides the nutrients necessary for good health. The U.S. Department of Agriculture suggests a diet of six to eleven servings of grain products (breads, cereals, pasta, and rice); three to five servings of various vegetables; two to four servings of various fruits; two to three servings of meat; and two to three servings of milk per day. Fats, oils, and sweets should be be used sparingly.
5. Psalm 37:4.
6. Be careful about paraphrases like *The Living Bible* and *The Message* because, although they might be helpful for gaining specific insights, they are not translations, but rather paraphrases. This means that the authors have taken certain liberties that may or may not communicate the writer's original intent to you.
7. Carol L. Otis, M.D., and Roger Goldingay, "Exercise Abuse—Have You Gone Too Far?" *Shape* magazine, October 1991, pp. 90-93.

Chapter 11—A Word Specifically for You

1. The concepts that I'm about to present to you here on the practice of labeling behavior will probably be new to you, so I'm asking that you hang in there and hear me out. Please try to judge what I say by Scripture—using God's revelation to determine truth.

A Biblical View of "Labels"

I have made a concerted effort in this book to give counsel that is founded upon Scripture. I've done this because I believe that Scripture contains all the truth that we need to know to please God. I know that there are many other ways, aside from biblically, to look at the difficulties we face in life, including a myriad of ways to address destructive eating patterns. Even those who say that they rely on Scripture may disagree with my views. I trust that those who disagree will go to Scripture to verify their beliefs.

Personally, I've sought to rely on Scripture alone because I believe it to be the only reliable standard whereby we can know what our problems are and how we can change our lives in ways that are pleasing to God. I recognize that I don't have the wisdom that you need—only God does.

The Problems with Medical-Sounding Labels

First, the use of labels (such as *bulimia* or *anorexia*) promotes the idea that one is sick with a *disease*. If you have been told that you are bulimic, for example, you might think that you have a *sickness* because you have been labeled with a medical-sounding name used in the medical community. "I have bulimia" may be used by some people in the same way as "I have diabetes." Instead of saying, "I practice bulimic behaviors," which is more accurate, you are encouraged to speak about these habits as though they were something over which you have no control—such as the progression of tuberculosis in your body.

This Isn't My Fault

I object to labeling behaviors *as diseases* because it might cause people who have been labeled in that way to think they are not responsible for the condition they are struggling with. If I am diagnosed with Multiple Sclerosis, for example, I probably wouldn't spend time thinking about how I was responsible to change the behavior that caused it. No, MS is not engendered by my behavior. The label "MS" (and all medical designations) are helpful and appropriate when describing certain somatic problems or organic abnormalities that impair normal physical functioning.

I Can't Help It

The use of labels also breeds excuse-making. A person who has been labeled in this way might think, *I can't help the fact that I'm starving myself...I have a disease...I'm anorexic,* or *I can't help eating this gallon of ice cream; I'm compulsive.* None of us needs any outside help in making excuses for our sinful behavior. Personally, I know that I'm pretty good at it on my own. Since the Bible teaches that we are responsible for our behavior, it would be wise to learn to differentiate between problems created by our own thoughts and actions and problems we face because of other factors.

Where Is the Hope?

I also object to the use of labels when describing behavior because I believe that it robs people of any hope for change. If I have a disease that has attacked me from without and is something that I had nothing to do with causing, then what can I do to stop its progression? Slowly, surely, it will have its way. I can try to slow it down, I can look for a cure, but . . . then what? "Excuses not only excuse, they condemn." Right now it may seem more palatable to think about your behavior as a disease over which you have no control—but then what? How will you be able to find the peace and joy that you long for? If, on the other hand, I realize that I willfully choose to practice a certain behavior, and this behavior is causing both spiritual and physiological problems, I can change my behavior and try to mitigate the collateral damage that is being done to my body.

I long for you to have hope that change *is* possible—that you haven't been saddled with some illness that will ravage your body and destroy you. I believe that you can change because I don't believe that compulsive overeating, bulimia, or anorexia are, in their essence, "diseases." They do cause physiological damage, to be sure. But I don't know of any scientific or medical proof that there are chemical agents, genes, viruses, or bacteria that *cause* these behaviors. Granted, I might have a genetic propensity (or hormone or brain chemical imbalances or allergies) toward obesity, but *I do not compulsively overeat because of it.* This physiological weakness might mean that I have to try harder to maintain a healthy weight, but that natural disposition toward "roundness" didn't make me a glutton. No, I choose to do that myself. It is devastating to call my gluttony an illness because in doing so I trick myself into thinking that my sin is not really sin—no, I have accepted a word that is more pleasant sounding—and have turned away from the only source of true heart-change, Jesus Christ. Remember, Jesus Christ died to save *sinners*.

Seeking Healing

Furthermore, if I think that I have a disease, then what will I need to do? Of course, I will need *healing*. And how will I obtain this healing? I might go from doctor to doctor, looking for some new medicine that would heal me—remember the phenfen debacle? Or, I might go from meeting to meeting, searching for someone with the faith to pray the right words to cast out my demons, to heal my sickness. The really tragic part of this searching is that once again it turns my attention away from the true help that is available from the power of the Holy Spirit as He sanctifies me. It focuses my faith on a weaker, less effective source. Please understand, I'm not saying that you shouldn't go to your doctor and use any legitimate scientific methods available. Nor am I saying that having your pastor or others pray for you is wrong. What I *am* saying is that God has laid out His method for our change very plainly in Scripture, and if we expect to receive His strength, we must follow His lead. The first step in doing this is to call our ungodly behaviors what He has called them, and then to seek to change by employing the methods He has chosen.

This Disease Makes Me Special

Finally, some women may take some sort of pride in being unique, different, a person with a serious disorder. For instance, Dr. Sue Baily, who is the director of the Eating Disorders Clinic at the Washington D.C. Hospital Center, says, "Bulimia almost has celebrity status, the 'in' thing to have." We need to fight the temptation to seek our identity in some label, and rather learn our identity from Scripture.

2. Farley, Dixie, *Eating Disorders: When Thinness Becomes an Obsession*, U.S. Food and Drug Administration, FDA Consumer, May 1986, internet article.

3. *Statistics Related to Overweight and Obesity*, National Institute of Health Publication No. 96-4158, July 1996.

4. The entire book of Judges is one repetition after another of this story. See Judges 2:11ff; 3:7,12; 4:1; 6:1; 10:6; 13:1. Psalm 78 also chronicles this cycle of idolatry, judgment, and repentance. See verses: 10-11, 17-18, 32, 34, 41, 56-58.

Chapter 12—Crossing the Finish Line

1. 1 Corinthians 7:34, and note the closing words.

2. Proverbs 14:12; 16:25.

3. Clarke, Adam, *Clarke's Commentary*, Electronic Database, Copyright 1996 by Biblesoft.